The DISCIPLINE of MASTERS

Scott Allan is an international bestselling author of 25+ books published in 7 languages in the area of personal growth and self-development. He is the author of *Fail Big, Undefeated,* and *Do the Hard Things First*.

As a former corporate business trainer in Japan, and Transformational Mindset Strategist, Scott has invested over 10,000 hours of research and instructional coaching into the areas of self-mastery and leadership training.

With an unrelenting passion for teaching, building critical life skills, and inspiring people around the world to take charge of their lives, Scott Allan is committed to a path of constant and never-ending self-improvement.

Many of the success strategies and self-empowerment material that is reinventing lives around the world evolves from Scott Allan's 20 years of practice and teaching critical skills to corporate executives, individuals, and business owners.

You can connect with Scott at:
scottallan@scottallanpublishing.com
Visit author.to/ScottAllanBooks to stay up to date on future book releases.

More Bestselling Titles From Scott Allan

Empower Your Thoughts

Empower Your Deep Focus

Rejection Reset

Rejection Free

Relaunch Your Life

Drive Your Destiny

The Discipline of Masters

Do the Hard Things First

Undefeated

No Punches Pulled

Fail Big

Bite the Bullet

Supercharge Your Best Life

Built for Stealth

Visit author.to/ScottAllanBooks to follow Scott Allan and stay up to date on future book releases

The DISCIPLINE *of* MASTERS

Destroy **Big Obstacles** and Become a **Bigger Leader**

SCOTT ALLAN

RUPA

Published by
Rupa Publications India Pvt. Ltd 2023
7/16, Ansari Road, Daryaganj
New Delhi 110002

Sales Centres:
Bengaluru Chennai
Hyderabad Jaipur Kathmandu
Kolkata Mumbai Prayagraj

P-ISBN: 978-93-5702-149-4
E-ISBN: 978-93-5702-150-0

First impression 2023

10 9 8 7 6 5 4 2 3 1

Printed in India

Contents

"Self-discipline is an act of cultivation. It requires you to connect today's actions to tomorrow's results. There's a season for sowing a season for reaping. Self-discipline helps you know which is which."

—Gary Ryan Blair

"The more aware of your intentions and your experiences you become, the more you will be able to connect the two, and the more you will be able to create the experiences of your life consciously. This is the development of mastery. It is the creation of authentic power."

— Gary Zukav

The Discipline of Masters

> *"People create their own success by learning what they need to learn and then by practicing it until they become proficient at it."*
>
> **— Brian Tracy**

Are you tired of being a slave to circumstances beyond your control? Lacking discipline and need a clear direction on how to be more productive, prolific and purpose-driven? Are you blocked by obstacles that stop your progress? Want to express your creativity through prolific ideas but not sure where to begin?

In that case, you are in the right place. I know why you are here. You are tired of feeling tired and looking for answers to a better way of living.

By being disciplined in the four key areas taught in this book, you can make massive changes in your life and the lives of others.

But first, a few words on mastery.

Why We Fail to Master Life

This book is titled *The Discipline of Masters* because it focuses on employing discipline as a means to achieve something greater than ourselves. By putting into practice the action steps you'll find at the end of each of these key areas, you will become more prolific in achieving your goals, become more focused, and condition your mindset to shift into a position of empowerment.

As we carve out our master vision for the life that can be, a new world of possibilities becomes available to us. You can get out of a bad marriage before it destroys you emotionally, or you can break away from a job that makes you miserable.

The path to becoming a Master of Discipline is about finding ways to suffer less by improving in the areas of life that can alleviate that suffering. You have the power of choice to turn your life into everything it could be. You also have the power to destroy your own potential through self-destructive behaviors. There are always two paths to go by.

For example, by overcoming your obstacles in life, you open up a clear pathway to become more creative. You spend less time engaged in bad habits and time-wasting activities. You complain less about others because you no longer concern yourself with the external drama going on around you. You realize that time is your most valuable commodity and you need to treat it better than gold. Instead of wasting it, you find ways to invest in your future by taking action in the moment.

The Discipline of Success in Four Key Areas

The Discipline of Masters focuses on accelerating your natural drive through a combination of four themes: overcoming obstacles, time mastery, leadership and mentoring, and the organization and implementation of creative ideas.

But more than that, it helps you master the core areas of your life that impact happiness, achievement, growth and creativity. You will learn to pivot your mindset and start moving in the direction intended for you to flow.

Once you take action in each of these core areas, you can be more creative, build greater confidence, be more productive and live the life you were born to lead.

Here is a breakdown of the book and the key benefits you will get on the inside:

Part 1: The Master of Destroying Obstacles

In this section, I will show you a step-by-step formula for tackling the four levels of self-defeat: Procrastination, fear, perfection and addiction. You will learn to break down your obstacles so they have less power over you.

It starts here with learning how to break down the big roadblocks in your way. As long as we are trapped within the model of self-defeat, we will never take charge of who we really are. Instead, we will end up with a broken, shattered existence.

Learn to master your circumstances by overcoming the roadblocks blocking you from getting to where you want to be. As we will see, you are unlimited in your potential. Now it is time to prove it.

Part 2: The Master of Time Investment

If you are wasting time, you waste your life. Learn the basics of managing your time so you get more out of your life. We waste hundreds of hours a month—excessive TV watching, games, shopping, online binging—and with this section, you can gain greater mastery over your time and your life.

By putting into practice time-management tools such as the Pomodoro technique and the 80/20 principle, you will be better equipped to manage your actions and, thus, have more time to spend on what matters most.

Part 3: The Master of Mentoring and Leadership

A mentor has a positive impact on the lives of many people. Do you have the desire to become a leader and a mentor, but you are not sure how? Do you follow the wrong people and need to become a mentor for the right people?

Mentoring is a valuable skill that allows us to help people achieve their greatest goals and aspire to reach the places they could never dream of.

As a mentor, you can help people get where they never imagined possible. Imagine working with someone and helping them to grow, explore, and, ultimately, succeed in an area of life they once dreamed of.

If you want to make an impact on the world, it begins with leading people and building a legacy that has impact. You can have influence on everyone that you connect with and be a source of inspiration for generations to come.

Part 4: The Master of Building Creative Ideas

How about all of those ideas swimming around in your head? Do you dismiss your ideas as silly or unrealistic? Your imagination is a powerhouse of wealth.

This is where a life is forged, within the reaches of your imagination, and this is where your greatest ideas can bring a dream to life. But how do you capture these ideas when they occur? How do you manage your thoughts and ideas to stay on track?

Don't lose the good stuff because you forgot to write it down. In this section, you will learn to capture your ideas and apply creativity to make positive changes. By keeping your ideas and turning them into a plan of action, you can develop new products or build the dream business you have always wanted. Imagine where your ideas could take you, and that is where you will end up.

Who Am I?

My name is Scott Allan, and I am a High Performance confidence coach and Mindset Optimization leader. For years I have been teaching people the strategies and techniques for destroying internal fears and overcoming the power of rejection that defeats them.

Since life is best served when we are chipping away at the obstacles in our lives that keep us stuck, I help thousands of people just like you to recover from the obstacles that defeat them through my books and coaching.

My mission is to provide you with the tools, life skills, and confidence to take control of your life.

I have struggled with failure and self-defeat for most of my life. Through addictions, negative behaviors, and a life of struggling to change bad habits, I have worked to overcome many obstacles on my journey toward freedom. So, just like you, I know what it is like to struggle and feel like you are spinning your wheels. I know what it is like to feel completely alone on the journey.

I know that change is not easy. If you have nobody giving you advice or guiding you along the way, it is easier to give in to the lesser path. I do not want you to give up; you deserve the best in life, and if you work on yourself just a little bit every day, you can experience the full benefits of what I am going to teach you. The time to take action is now.

Even if you have a strong desire to break your limitations, this will not happen until you disengage the core negativities that are keeping you stuck. Thanks to the techniques I am going to share with you in this book, you can begin to live the life that you have always dreamed of but could never quite reach.

You see, if we are not in charge of our lives, someone or something else is. If we are not making choices that empower us, we are making choices that limit us. I have made a lot of progress because of the wisdom and teachings past mentors shared with me. I want to share this wisdom with you now in The Discipline of Masters.

Why This Book Is a Good Fit for You

In this book, you will learn to:

- Confront the fear of big obstacles blocking your growth
- Identify and eliminate your greatest self-defeating behavior
- Remove the quick-fix addiction cycle
- Challenge old beliefs holding you prisoner
- Confront the habit of procrastination and learn to do it NOW
- Focus on life design instead of life crisis
- Navigate the ten pillars of delegating important work
- Create a system for capturing your prolific ideas

Life mastery is about focusing in on the specific areas of your life that deliver impact. Your habits, actions, and ability to concentrate play large roles in conditioning your mind to stay on track.

Now ask yourself...

- How would your life be different if you no longer gave in to quick-fix short cuts?
- How prolific could you be from this moment forward if you made every minute count?
- What level could you aspire to if you showed others how to be their best through mentorship or coaching?
- What would happen if you paid more attention to your creative genius and blended your ideas with creative passion?
- What area of your life matters most to you right now, and how would your life take on massive change if you focused in on this area?

Think about the possibilities. Let go of any self-imposed short-term limitations. Release your internal fear and take action moving forward.

The time is now to build something real that counts toward the big picture. Take action today so you are always moving the needle in a progressive direction.

We have a lot of content to cover in a short amount of time. I recommend you keep a notebook handy and take notes. There are lots of strategies and key tactics I share in this book, and I don't want you to miss anything.

Ready?

Turn the page and let's begin the training.

Scott A

Section I: The Master of Destroying Obstacles

"Obstacles are placed in your path to prepare you for a higher purpose. These physical and mental roadblocks challenge you to rise to new levels of responsibility. To overcome your greatest limitations is to overcome the imperfections of the ego-mind holding you prisoner. You must face what you fear and work to overcome the obstacles that stand between you and all your hopes and dreams. You may come to realize, after all is won, that the biggest obstacle in your path is yourself."

— Scott Allan

Pathways to Self-defeat

"Obstacles will look large or small to you according to whether you are large or small."

— Orison Swett Marden

Hell is the place where our mental, physical, and emotional faculties are at the mercy of uncontrollable habits and destructive behavior patterns. These obstacles separate the achievement of lifelong dreams from bitter failures, turning our lives into either a heaven or a purgatory.

Self-defeating behaviors—referred to in this book as SDBs—are barriers of defeat that act as internal coping mechanisms, usually cultivated from a young age. As our dependency on these behaviors grows in strength, we unintentionally nurture an addictive cycle providing us with instant pleasure and relief from our pain.

Over the years of repetitive practice, these behaviors become integrated into our lifestyle and threaten to rob us of everything we stand for.

As our lives become unstructured and we lose sight of what matters most, a self-destructive cycle begins to take shape. Our lives become altered and twisted, forging a string of pathways that eventually lead to a chain of self-defeating habits.

We have a hard time accepting that our self-defeating habits were created by us, and when we can tap into this level of self-awareness, we will then realize they are destroyed by us as well. It is one thing to be defeated by someone, but it is another to be defeated by yourself.

This is a critical point to take in: most people are defeated by their own actions and not the actions of others. While the actions of others impact us, it is our reaction to the crisis that determines whether we can get through it.

When faced with a threatening situation or trauma, our natural instinct is to resort to the emotional and mental relief that these quick-fix behaviors bring us. In the beginning, self-defeating behaviors appear to be the best friends you could ever have. But in the end, they are exposed for the fake imposters of deception that they are.

SDBs are disguised as loyal companions: dependable, trustworthy, and predictable. They are always there when we need them. And because they predictably numb our pain, helping us to avoid facing an unpleasant truth or situation, our dependency on these behaviors runs deeper and becomes more internalized over time.

Self-defeating behaviors are manifested as mild to extreme mental and emotional ailments, an internal sickness of the mind and body that can harm us physically, mentally, emotionally, and spiritually, often placing us in danger through unlawful or spontaneous compulsive actions.

They destroy all our chances for expressing love, achieving success, having wealth, or taking control of our lives. As long as we are trapped within the model of self-defeat, we will never take charge of who we really are. We will never seize the day or become masters of our universe. Instead, we will end up with a broken, shattered existence.

Let's not let that happen.

These behaviors may appear in the form of addictions, negative thinking, and personality disorders, as well as destructive actions. They corrupt personal relationships through hatred, anger, jealousy, envy, fear, greed, manipulation, addiction, or self-centeredness. SDBs are the internal weeds that have grown out of control in the garden of the mind.

It is a repetitive cycle trapping you in a world of lies and deceit, and the more these cycles are allowed to continue, the more likely you will always operate within a state of complete unawareness.

Self-defeating behaviors work because they are reliable and produce the instant results you need. Deceptive in nature, SDBs appear as last-minute saviors to rid you of a situation you don't want to deal with, helping to numb the pain through alternative methods and providing you, the victim, with weaker choices that appear like the only way out.

We get hooked on the instant relief and escape from emotional pain and trauma that SDBs provide, even if the escape is only momentary. It is these weak emotional lapses that are conditioned to respond to behaviors of crisis whenever we experience any form of stress, pressure, or fatigue.

It is this place where you have stored your worst nightmares, negative behaviors, and buried skeletons of the past. It is also the birthplace of all character defects and cracks in your psyche, which provide the starting point for these defeating behaviors to grow and develop.

A Price to Pay

There is a price to pay for using and abusing a behavior of self-defeat. In the beginning, SDBs give us everything we want, but eventually turn on us, their masters, to deliver a lethal injection. Nothing comes for free, and your behaviors of chaos carry a heavy price in the end.

There is the alcoholic that once enjoyed drinking, until one day they have no friends or family.

The gambler that loses everything, but still continues the downward spiral, borrowing money from friends, family, and coworkers.

The compulsive shopper that has no spending limits, despite owing thousands to creditors and banks.

The manipulators and cheats; the compulsive and impulsive people; and, the people struggling with the inevitable various addictive patterns and feelings of hopelessness that come from not facing the obstacles, problems, and demons that challenge them on a daily basis.

"Don't let fear or insecurity stop you from trying new things. Believe in yourself. Do what you love. And most importantly, be kind to others, even if you don't like them."

— Stacy Landon

Eventually, the price for engaging in this behavior is much heavier than we ever expected. What you must do is take a look at yourself and your current state, analyze these unhealthy and disruptive behaviors, and identify those behaviors when they start to occur.

Self-defeating behaviors are the symptoms of unresolved issues within ourselves, and although further therapy or support beyond what I can offer you here may be required, you should at least learn to recognize where, when, and how you are trapped in a cycle of self-defeat. This usually occurs when we lack certain life skills and coping mechanisms to defend ourselves against the personal weaknesses that plague the heart and mind.

Know now that recovery and a fresh start to building a better life is a choice only you can make. Instead of paying a heavy price for your suffering, you have the power of choice to determine your own personal value.

You can make your actions count by choosing to do so. You will move from a place of feeling useless and unworthy to a place of maximizing your personal worth by severing the cycle of destructive power these behaviors create.

An Attachment to Pain

Self-defeating behaviors are difficult to remove because of the attachment we have placed on them. Negative behaviors act as high walls keeping us safe from the world but are, in fact, the prison of our lives. Instead of keeping us safe, they force us into further isolation.

Your self-defeating behaviors are powerful because you made them that way. You have trained your behaviors to react in a certain way to situations that you find undesirable.

Instead of facing the pain and jumping the hurdles to overcome an obstacle, we have discovered that it is easier to avoid it, to go around it without confronting it, or to retreat from it. The lesson we have learned is that the things we run from eventually catch up to us.

Emotionally, mentally, physically, and socially, we have formed an attachment to SDBs that keeps them around. But how do you rid yourself of something that feels so much a part of you that ridding yourself of it would feel like cutting off a limb or giving up one of your organs?

Without our coping mechanisms, we are conned into believing we are nothing, like children standing naked in the forest, surrounded by hungry lions. To remove the addictive patterns of defeat would be like tearing down the walls of uncertainty, leaving us vulnerable and without any support system.

It is the fear that, even if you do rid yourself of the self-defeating behaviors that have protected you for so long, you won't be able to handle life when it throws you a new problem.

In that situation, you look for something to help you through it, and that might be an addiction, a new relationship, or an outburst of sudden, violent anger.

Self-defeating behaviors win because we have concluded that although we can't live with them, we certainly can't live without them.

These patterns of chaos threaten to take away everything we hope to gain, detaining our best efforts and throwing a dark blanket of doubt, insecurity, low self-esteem and helplessness over any chance for success. Doing battle with the demons hibernating within is not a war that most people are willing to engage in.

We would rather face hunger or a torture rack than have to deal with the enemy that lives inside. But this is where the real healing begins, and only those with the determination to rise up again and again will be able to face the darker parts of themselves and the obstacles and fears blocking their path to healing and recovery.

Taking Back Control

The nature of our negative behaviors is control. As long as they are in control, you are not. SDBs, once they've established a pattern of habits, burrow deep within the conscious mind and stay there until called for. Without realizing it, these patterns of self-defeat take total control of our lives.

We know something isn't right, but we just can't seem to point out what it could be. SDBs are well versed in manipulating the mind; they disguise themselves in dark shadows of fear and self-doubt, twisting reality into so many variations that you can no longer separate the truth from the lie.

It is here where you need to take a stand. It is time to step up and gain control of your life. You are not a victim of circumstances; you are the creator of circumstances. You are not a weak individual, but someone with great strength and unlimited potential for achieving great things.

Your self-defeating behaviors do not own you or control you. Once you decide to take affirmative action, SDBs start to lose their power over you and eventually wither away. The challenges ahead are not on an easy path to follow. To achieve this goal, it takes commitment, a desire to recover, and a willingness to go to any lengths necessary.

Knowing your true self begins with confronting the dark shadows of unresolved painful issues. The road to hell is a personal struggle with the defects of a flawed character.

Throughout the course of your lifetime, you will face your self-defeating behaviors and deep character flaws so you can become the person you always dreamed about. By confronting your worst demons, you will be successful in overcoming your SDBs.

You must take a stand against the barriers that hold you back. To smash through the roadblocks and obstacles of your worst fears is to rise to a new level of mental, emotional, and spiritual perfection.

You don't have to be a victim of past events or suffer the cycle of defeat that has corrupted your way of life. You have the resources to fight back! You have everything you need to get anything you want. It is time to expose your lies to the truth. It is time to be free.

> *"Obstacles can't stop you. Problems can't stop you. Most of all, other people can't stop you. Only you can stop you."*
>
> **— Jeffrey Gitomer**

SDBs appear to save the day but are, in fact, the villains of a much darker truth—a truth that conceals an even darker wall of lies. The more you feed into your behaviors of defeat, the taller the walls around your world are. These behaviors get you to buy into the idea that if you want to feel better about yourself, this is the easiest and most reliable path to take.

Once you make a pact with your self-defeating behavior of choice, you have entered into a contract with a double-edged blade. On the one side, a self-defeating behavior provides the necessary means to escape or avoid painful situations. It removes you from reality and replaces it with a false sense of security. It provides what you need in the beginning and wraps its victim—you—in a protective blanket of illusion.

When the day comes that you no longer benefit from or see the need for such behaviors to continue, you will realize they are not going to leave so easily, certainly not after you have invested so much of your time and energy into their growth.

The problem is, however, that self-defeating behaviors can only offer you a short-term fix, but they have a long-life cycle, stretching over the course of your life for years and even decades, keeping you blocked off from achieving your true potential and burying the truth underneath a mountain of lies and false beliefs.

We live in a quick-fix world that focuses on short-term solutions. In an attempt to deal with the pain of life through weak coping mechanisms, society has built up a dependency on alternate sources to get through the crises of life. Our world has become addicted to the temporary fix instead of focusing on long-term solutions that last.

The Nature of the Beast

A self-defeating behavior, whether or not it is an addiction or a mental ailment brought on by high, developed stress, has the unique ability to hibernate—it will transform itself from one form to another through adopting various behaviors and lay dormant in order to avoid being detected.

When called upon, it will rise to the occasion and take action. The inevitable result in the long run can only be a deeper failure beyond the realm of anything you have ever experienced. Believe me when I tell you that the pain that you avoid today will only magnify itself over time.

I can tell you this: the only path to freedom is the path through hell. Self-defeating behaviors are but symptoms of the problems we have and failing to address them is to fail completely.

Everyone is attached to at least one behavior that defeats them on a continual basis. Whether you are aware of it or not, you have at least one obstacle in your life, even if it is a subtle one, hindering your mental and spiritual growth and feeding your actions and choices with negative influence.

Self-defeat focuses on the moment and provides just enough relief to keep us coming back for more.

It becomes like a drug, and the more of it you use, the more of it you need to keep getting the results required to survive the moment. It becomes a mad circle of unhealthy patterns, a crazed merry-go-round that never stops long enough for you to escape.

It is the nature of the beast to keep you on the ride as long as possible, providing no way out and blocking all roads to recovery.

The Four Levels of Self-Defeat

"Success is not measured by what you accomplish, but by the opposition you have encountered, and the courage with which you have maintained the struggle against overwhelming odds."

— Orison Swett Marden

In order to recognize the behaviors defeating you, you need to understand how they take control of our lives. The four levels described here are: fear, procrastination, perfection, and addiction.

Fear: The First Obstacle of Defeat

A set of self-created fantasies, consisting of the worst-case scenarios imaginable, believed to be coming true.

Our fears are self-created prophecies of doom and gloom appearing to us as real-life situations. They are false perceptions of reality that paint a grim picture of how we believe the future will turn out, and when we believe in these fears, they become real. When you believe in fear, you create fear, setting a course for either a life of success or bitter failure.

The Shape of Fear

Fear molds and shapes the course of life in many ways. Fears can empower you to become more than you are, or it enslaves you to diminish any chances for success at all. Fear is a powerful emotional state of mind. When you are in control of your emotions and mental state, you acquire the personal power to take control of any fear-based thoughts you are having.

The ability to work with and manage your fear so it is no longer your enemy but instead becomes your ally is possible through recognizing the things, events, and people that make you fearful. Remember this: you can't hide from your fear; you must take immediate action and do the things you are afraid to do. Only then will you experience the true meaning of freedom.

Remember that the fear you experience in any situation will never go away. You will never be rid of fear because when faced with a new problem or challenge, you will most likely experience fear as part of the natural course. Learn to accept this truth, and then you can take the steps necessary to live with it and adopt it as an ally rather than an enemy.

Below are some of the areas that we can focus on to shape our fears, using them as powerful tools that work for us rather than against.

Fear shapes thoughts.

Unconditioned fear produces fearful thoughts that lead to negative thinking and another pathway to self-defeat. Thoughts that are fear-based infect every aspect of your life—your self-esteem, self-confidence, willpower to take action, opportunity, and ability to visualize goals clearly.

When we are trapped in the negative thought patterns of uncontrolled fear, we create a mental paralysis that fuels self-defeat.

Fear shapes mental attitude

It is not the events that shape our lives, but rather our attitude toward those events. If your fears are allowed to take over and turn every situation into a frightening experience, your mental attitude will weaken, bringing unwanted results and disempowering your life in many ways.

Work to build up your mental attitude into a powerful, positive state and maintain control over the thoughts that influence the mental condition. People with a healthy and well-conditioned mental attitude are rarely affected or frightened by fear. They know they can handle anything thrown their way.

Fear shapes success

There is the myth that in order to be successful at anything, you have to first get rid of the fear blocking your path. This is true to some extent, but it is your association with your deepest fears and not facing up to your traumas that have kept you frozen in place.

Depending on your relationship with fear, you can create the best or the worst of worlds. Success is about overcoming your fears and learning to live with the fear you do have. When you confront a fear and rid yourself of the power it has over you, your real success begins to take shape. Every time you act in the face of your fear, when you take control over the devices that keep you trapped, that is the victory.

Remember that fear is not always a bad thing. The more you work to control it, the more you can use it to your advantage. For example, perhaps your biggest self-defeating fear is the fear of not having any money.

You can feed into this fear by believing in it, thus keeping an abundance of money away from you. Or you can take charge and figure out a way to increase your income, either through business investments, a strong financial portfolio, or taking a personal financial course.

The key to having success over fear is action. Sometimes the fear of not having or of losing something is a powerful motivator encouraging you to go after it. Fear is a road sign that points you in the direction of success. If you follow it, you will encounter that fear, and when you do, you will realize it was there to prompt you to take action.

Fear shapes beliefs

The experiences we have create many of our beliefs. If those experiences were perceived as frightful or harmful, we develop a phobia surrounding the fear to try to avoid repeating that experience at all costs. Everyone has something they fear, and this fear begins with your belief in something that is harmful, dangerous, or a threat.

Remember that what you believe in becomes your reality. If you believe in the fears that govern your life and control your actions, this is the reality you create for yourself. The things you positively believe in are attracted to you. The things you fear the most are also attracted to you. Change your fear-based beliefs and you can shift the possible negative outcome of any situation into a positive experience.

Solutions for Handling the Fear

Solution #1: Imagine the best outcome possible. You have to believe in the life you want to own. If it is our habit to imagine the worst possible situations coming true, we become so distracted that we can't see all that our life has to offer. When all you imagine and think about are catastrophic endings, you create the exact results and situations you fear coming true.

This stems from one of the great laws of attraction: what we perceive to be real ultimately is real. When you believe in your fears, you create your fears. From this moment on, focus on the best possible outcome for any situation, no matter how hopeless a situation appears to be at that moment. Imagine the situation you want to create, and not the scenario that your fear-based mind is feeding to you.

Solution #2: Challenge the beliefs holding you prisoner. The most fearful events of all are imagined ones. We imagine over and over again the terrifying events that are going to take place. We obsess about them, think about them, and try to invent ways that will stop the worst from coming true by avoiding all risks whatsoever. In the process, many of us end up avoiding living our lives once the fear becomes so bad.

Inevitably, you are creating the situations allowing these disasters to occur. Remember, most fear is an illusion of disbelief that we are convinced is the truth. This is how fear starts to build itself up. It starts as something small at one point, and through the habitual practice of consistent fear building, events that never take place blossom into uncontrollable fantasies of terror.

Take charge and challenge your irrational beliefs and thoughts. Think about what would happen if the worst event imaginable really did occur. Often it is not the fear of what will happen that scares us the most; rather, it is the doubt of our own ability to handle the situation when and if it does happen. We are afraid of ourselves, afraid that we won't be able to find a solution to deal with a fearful situation when it happens.

Perhaps you fear losing your job, in which case you might be more terrified of the prospect of having to find another job. It is our fear of having to face the fear that immobilizes us. What if I fail? What if can't handle it? What if I can handle it, and then I am given further responsibility?

Well, you can handle it. Act as if it has already happened. Instead of being afraid of it happening, accept that it will happen, and that now you have to confront it head on. Train your mind to handle anything that comes your way. Fear keeps you immobilized; action mobilizes you.

Solution #3: Educate yourself about fear. One of the greatest discoveries I ever made about fear is that the more you know about what causes your fear, the less afraid you are and the more manageable your fears become.

Fear is often created through the absence of knowledge. Get to know your fears by learning about them, studying them, and trying to trace them back to their origins. Every fear has a point of origin. Trace your fears back to their point of origin and you will unravel a great mystery.

Find resources on your fears and read about the people that have overcome the same fears you are now experiencing. Copy the techniques and tools they used to manage their fears and apply them to your own life. If one technique doesn't work right away, try another, and keep trying different methods of fear removal until you find the one that works for you.

<u>Solution #4:</u> Replace the negative with the positive. This is a process I like to call swapping. Your fears have been conditioned to respond to certain situations that you find threatening. However, if you follow the advice in the previous technique, you will be able to take those negative reactions and turn them into positive ones.

Negativity is a conditioned response. You were not born this way. You learned to be negative, probably through your own failures to measure up to the expectations of others and yourself, or through watching others closest to you, like your parents, deal poorly with their own problems.

One of the ways to win over the negativity fear produces is to turn a negative thought or belief into a positive one as soon as it occurs. If you suddenly have the thought this isn't going to work out, turn that thought around immediately. Tell yourself, it is all working out right now, just as it should. I have control over this. Continue this method of thought control until turning over your fearful, negative thoughts becomes second nature.

Two Sides of the Fear-Based Mind

Remember that for every fear you have, you are also afraid of the opposite. If you fear failure, chances are you fear the complete opposite of failure, which would be success. If you fear rejection, you also fear being accepted. Likewise, fear of change invokes a fear of staying the same, or staying in a rut, or of not making progress in your life.

It is a catch-22 scenario. You feel damned if you do and damned if you don't. You feel completely immobile, unable to move, or take any action whatsoever; every step is an intense effort. Let's take a look at some of these fears below that have had a chokehold on your life.

Identifying our fears is the first step to working out a system for managing them. Below is a list of the fears we create through our experiences and imagination. Check the fears that have had an impact on your life. Imagine yourself living without this fear. What would you do? How would you behave? What actions would you take if the fear was not controlling you?

Make a list of the disadvantages and roadblocks that each fear poses. See how many of your own fears you can add to this list.

- Fear of failure and/or success
- Fear of responsibility
- Fear of love and intimacy
- Fear of rejection and/or being accepted
- Fear of being poor and/or rich (money-based fears)
- Fear of making mistakes (see Perfection)
- Fear of being judged
- Fear of people

- Fear of changing and/or staying the same
- Fear of ailments and sickness

Now, take some time to answer these questions about fear.

1. What negative impact have these fears had on your life?
2. What positive impact have these fears had on your life?
3. What are the advantages/disadvantages to holding on to these fears? On a sheet of paper, draw a line down the center and label the left half Advantages of Fear and, on the right side, Disadvantages of Fear.
4. If there were one fear that you could eliminate right now, what would it be? How has this fear controlled your life? What will happen if it continues to dominate your choices? Mind map your solutions and decide to implement the best choice.

Procrastination: The Second Obstacle of Defeat

A disagreeable challenge, task, problem or work that is put off for an undetermined length of time in order to avoid the pain or discomfort of having to work through it.

Procrastination, or task avoidance, is a defensive technique used to escape from the pain and unpleasantness of having to perform an undesirable task. This is a habit of escape used to get out of doing something that has been linked to your mind as an activity that is dull, boring, or—in some cases—plain terrifying.

The Cost of Procrastination

It is a vicious game we play with ourselves while we dance around our feelings of fear, criticism, self-loathing, low self-esteem, and guilt associated with our behaviors. The self-defeating behavior of task avoidance is a defense mechanism to escape reality, and as long as we have something to remove attention from our responsibilities, we won't have to face the pain of dealing with the burden of an unwanted situation.

Procrastination costs your valuable time, money, and self-esteem, and if continued over a lifetime, the end cost is the life you could have had but never did. Task avoidance catches up with you, and the things you try to avoid will only pile up, higher and higher, until you can't see over the mountain of stuff bogging down your life.

Even the smallest of jobs must be done, and if they are not done by you, they have to be done by someone else. This puts your responsibility on other people: friends, family, coworkers, and even people you don't know have to clean up after you.

Procrastination is a game that affects everyone, not just you, and this is something we must come to realize if we are to overcome this pattern of putting off life.

What Leads to Task Avoidance?

A person who is in the habit of procrastinating will either avoid starting something or will fail to finish something, often quitting halfway through. Procrastination emerges out of associating pain with the activity you know must be done.

One of the fears associated with procrastinating is trying something different. The thought of taking that first leap into the unknown causes most people to just stand on the edge and gaze into the great abyss rather than taking a leap of faith. For the person who is accustomed to putting off those things they want to avoid, they freeze at the thought of failing under harsh criticism.

This problem can be overcome by taking small steps. Instead of being overwhelmed by a project or task, break it up into small pieces and tackle each piece of the project in stages.

Consider each part of the task as a piece to a much larger whole. People have achieved their dreams through this easy process of breaking down difficult, lengthy tasks or work-related projects. You can, too.

> *"Procrastination is like a credit card:*
> *it's a lot of fun until you get the bill."*
>
> **— Christopher Parker**

A Short Exercise

Now, before reading any further, take a moment and write down a job or project that you have been avoiding. Write it out in big letters at the top of the page.

Next, brainstorm a list of small actions you are going to take to start working on this project. Is it a phone call? Filling out a form? Doing a bit of research online?

Write down as many of the steps you can think of that will start things moving in a positive direction. Now, choose one of the actions on the list. This is the first step you are going to do right now. After it has been completed, cross it of the list and choose another small task.

Remember this: The more action you take, the more momentum you create!

The "Someday" Strategy

People who avoid those things that should be done have one common trait inherent in almost every thought they have: they believe in a magical tomorrow, where everything they plan to do and have been avoiding for the last several months or years is somehow going to get done on this special day.

Of course, tomorrow eventually shows up, a lot sooner than was expected, and because you are not yet ready to start, everything gets pushed back to the next day.

This is the inherent cycle of procrastination, and the basic foundation for this behavior that robs people of their very lives. It is a belief that someday we will get our lives together. Someday I will think about my future. Someday I will take a chance and write that book, take that course, or go on that trip. Someday turns out to be forever!

It is a natural path we take to avoid unpleasant things. Life is full of things we would rather not do, activities that we view as a waste of time but must be done in order to make progress and continue to grow. Take care of things as they come up, and if you can't do it right away for lack of information or resources, make sure it gets done when the time is right.

To help you with this, I have included two techniques for getting you started on the road to action recovery. I would also recommend you read The Procrastinator's Handbook by Rita

Emmett or The Now Habit by Dr. Neil Fiore for further insight into defeating and managing procrastination.

Managing Procrastination

Make a task/activity avoidance list. Create a list of jobs, tasks, or projects you have been meaning to "get around to" but just haven't found the time.

Write down everything you possibly can, no matter how big or small, and create a list of activities, chores, jobs, and tasks that have piled up in your to-do pile. Then, once you have your list compiled, select the activities or jobs you are going to tackle first.

Choose a task, stick with it, get it done, and move on to the next one. The key is to create the feeling that you are making progress, even if it is a small step. One step ahead is better than both feet stuck indefinitely in the same spot.

Break it down. If it is a project that will take time, break it down into manageable chunks. Focus on one task at a time. Remember, if feeling overwhelmed is one of your avoidance triggers, you don't want to start several things at once.

You may have avoided some activities because the overall size of the project causes you to feel swamped or crushed under the weight of doing too many things. The job appears too large to your mind, so it seeks ways to avoid doing it. You see the project as one big whole. It's like you are standing at the bottom of the world's tallest mountain, looking up and wondering how am I going to ever climb this?

Now, imagine yourself standing at the bottom of that mountain looking up, and suddenly, every couple hundred feet or so you see rest stations where you can catch your breath, have a coffee, and build up your energy before the long trek to the next ledge.

Suddenly, what first seemed like an impossible journey is looking more and more manageable as you make progress, advancing by stages. Each ledge you come to brings you closer to your goal, until you eventually reach your destination.

Every challenge, project, or journey at first appears as a small speck on the horizon, but what brings it closer is taking that first step. And then another step, and then another. You will get there through steady progress, but you won't get anywhere if you remain frozen in place, terrified to move.

Remember—*The journey of a thousand miles is completed one step at a time.*

Perfection: The Third Obstacle of Defeat

The obsession to be perfect in all things; to perform flawlessly in all areas of life; to possess unrealistic expectations through the expectation of perfection in all matters.

People spend their lives trying to accomplish the impossible task of creating the perfect life and the perfect world. It is the obsession to be perfect in all things, to perform flawlessly in all areas of life, to possess unrealistic expectations through the expectation of perfection in all matters.

A Perfect World

The relentless pursuit of perfection often leads to a road of bitter disappointments, frustration, and grief—as the perfectionist realizes their goals are impossible to reach, their destination is always just out of reach, and what they seek is an illusion of hard-core beliefs that never seem to remain consistent.

The perfectionist believes in a world that must be perfect, and they apply all their energy and resources into creating the perfect environment, the perfect career, the perfect way of life. Perfectionism is a powerful disillusion; it is the ultimate lie. It does not exist but in the minds of those that pursue it with relentless obsession.

Perfectionists live in a world of black and white, an all-or-nothing way of thinking that fuels the belief that every small detail has to have the indelible seal of perfection stamped on it. There is no middle road and no forgiveness of self (or others) for errors or failure.

"Practice means to perform, over and over again in the face of all obstacles, some act of vision, of faith, of desire. Practice is a means of inviting the perfection desired."

— Martha Graham

Perfectionists either succeed beyond the norm or they fail miserably; something is either flawless, or it is seriously flawed. There are no mediocre results or "good efforts" in this game; there is no middle ground.

Perfectionism can be an obsessive mental disorder sustained by the fear of failure, low self-esteem, and the pursuit of a perfect world order that can never measure up to the high standards it demands. It is an illusion that always remains just out of reach.

Three Core Characteristics of the Perfectionist

1. Perfectionists live in a world of unattainable goals.

No mountain surmounted is ever high enough. A goal achieved, no matter how significant, is rarely appreciated because the perfectionist is already focused on reaching a higher plateau.

The struggle to attain these super-goals leaves many frustrated and depressed as their over-ambition becomes a dark cloud of self-disappointment. There is nothing more tragic than achieving something worthwhile and not taking the time to savor the victory.

2. Perfectionists hold to a system of unrelenting standards.

The core of perfection is the high level of expectations perfectionists have set for themselves and others. The people you associate with will fear not being able to live up to your demands.

Even for those that do, they can't maintain the same level of expectations you demand and soon fail under your scrutiny. It is because of this one applicable trait that most perfectionists find themselves alone, struggling against a world of indifference.

3. Perfectionists are highly critical of their self and others.

A true perfectionist passes judgment easily, especially when others disappoint or just don't measure up to expectations. Perfectionists are extremely unforgiving, especially when they talk to themselves. As someone once described it to me: "It is like there is a committee inside my head all day long, and I can't turn it off."

Perfect people use criticism as a means of keeping others in line, especially themselves. Perfectionists tend to be highly critical and are themselves extremely sensitive to criticism. They can deliver it but have a roadblock when it comes to receiving it. Nothing is more threatening to the perfectionist than the suggestion that they might be flawed or defective in some way.

Everything Is Flawed

Chances are if the perfectionist trap is one of the behaviors holding you back, you probably have derived an immense pleasure-gain from this. But the fact is that everything in life is flawed. The people, places, and things around you have real flaws.

When you shop for a new car and admire the beauty of its new paint; the perfect new engine underneath the nice, shiny hood; and the perfect smell of the fresh interior, remember that as you are forking over thousands of dollars for a piece of mint-looking machinery, this beautiful thing has flaws.

No matter how clean it looks, how much it costs, or how sophisticated it appears to be, there are flaws, and although they are not obviously transparent, they do exist.

A flaw is God's guarantee that there is always room to be better. Nothing is created without having flaws; every living creature—plants, trees, even the most sophisticated and intelligent species on our planet—is flawed in some way. The only real, perfect thing is an imperfection.

Addiction: The Fourth Obstacle of Defeat

A habitual disease of the mind and/or body that is deeply infected with the mental/physical attraction to foreign substances or actions that inevitably lead to out-of-control behavior through repeated patterns of abuse.

In our world today, there is an epidemic of disastrous proportions spreading into every town, community, and home. It is perhaps the most destructive of all self-defeating behaviors: the addiction cycle—a behavior of complete defeat, a master manipulator that has stolen our freedom and replaced it with the iron bars of an emotional and spiritual sickness.

The Road to Failure

Addiction is an affliction of the mind, affecting the addicted person in all manners of the physical, mental, emotional, and spiritual forms that make up the pillars of one's life. Struggling with addiction is like trying to run a race with a lead ball and chain tied to your leg: you might be able to drag the lead ball for a short distance, but sooner or later, you will collapse.

An addiction is a temporary loss of sanity. The one addicted becomes so completely preoccupied with the obsession that the only form of relief is to act out and give in to the demands of the addiction. It is more than just a bad habit: it is an obsession of the mind that once it has established a pattern of "pain relief," continues indefinitely unless there is an intervention, such as complete abstinence through recovery, hospitalization, or death.

"No one is immune from addiction; it afflicts people of all ages, races, classes, and professions."

— Patrick J. Kennedy

Addiction is an invisible thread of power that leads the addict down a long, winding, dark road, isolating them from friends and family until the addict has traveled to the point of no return. The only way back is to seek the help of people who have dealt with this form of insanity and have come back from the bottom of hell to tell their stories.

The secret to addiction recovery lies in the desire of the addict. If you truly have a desire to change and recover from your addiction, this is the starting point from which recovery is possible. It is simply not enough to stop something for a short period time or to only cut back on the destructive pattern of abuse.

The only cure is abstinence, a complete removal of the pattern and the substance or action fueling the addiction. Your goal is to break this cycle of defeat so you can stop the suffering and humiliation that comes with the disease. There can be no half measures with addiction. If you truly suffer from this disease, complete abstinence is the only solution.

Here are some of the more common addictions and suggestions for handling each addiction. I recommend that you become very familiar with your addiction through your own research. There are plenty of books and volumes on each of these addictive behaviors to make you an expert in the area of addictive behavior that affects you.

- Alcohol and drug addiction: includes all those drug-related addictions that influence your mental and physical state.
- Sex and relationship addiction: includes all sex-related addictions, as well as codependency.

- Gambling/spending/consumerism addiction: includes all financial-related addictions that lead to debt and financial hardship.
- Tobacco addiction: includes the consumption of nicotine (through cigarettes or other means).
- Addictive fillers: includes caffeine, chocolate, sugar, and all other substances that are used to fill up the individual with a sugar or caffeine high.

Tactics for Addiction Recovery

Addictions are severe aliments of the mind and soul that, if untreated, eventually result in the breakdown of the physical and mental condition. Even the seemingly less harmful addictions can, over time, have a powerful impact on your life. Here are some suggestions for building a path to recovery.

Meeting places. The Twelve-Step Program is now synonymous with recovery as a set of guiding principles for addiction recovery. If you are going to be successful at defeating and keeping your addiction under control, both the Twelve-Step Program and working with others that have the same affliction are proven best methods to a successful recovery.

The twelve steps lay out a plan for recovery in such a way that anyone can do them with the help and support of a friend or sponsor. I highly recommend doing them with someone, such as a counselor or sponsor, who has experience and can walk you through the steps to recovery; the advice you receive from another could prove invaluable to your success in recovery.

In addition to working through the twelve steps, it is important to go to the place where people with addictions hang out. This would be meeting places set up for discussing and learning to understand the nature of your addiction.

Decades ago, little was known about addictive personalities. Today, however, there are thousands of meetings a week in big cities and small towns across America and all around the world. Nobody has to suffer alone anymore, as it is the nature of addiction to isolate the addict, making the person dependent and helpless. Through the steps and attending meetings, you are fighting back and gaining the control over your life that you once only dreamed of.

Avoid trigger spots. If you are working toward alcohol abstinence, it would be wise to avoid establishments that serve alcohol. Your trigger spots could take you right back to where you used to be.

A nicotine addict should abstain from hanging around people who are still smoking, the sex addict should abstain from hanging around the adult section of the bookstore, and the person with an eating disorder might have to avoid the all-you-can-eat menu.

Avoiding trigger spots and knowing what and where these places are, as well as the times of day your triggers usually work, is essential to recovery. If you don't know what your triggers are, you will after only a couple of weeks in recovery.

Triggers are encouraged by certain places, specific times of day, and certain individuals that play a role in the repeated relapse of the one suffering from addiction. Remember that addiction is an illness, and, like most illnesses, you have to take precautions to avoid putting yourself at further risk.

Whether or not it is a bar, casino, the internet, or the junk food section of the supermarket, work to know and understand how your addiction operates. What are the things that feed it and give it its power? Once you figure this out, recognizing and dealing with your trigger areas will become second nature.

The Road Home: Your Path to Recovery

Facing your destructive behaviors of chaos is one of the greatest challenges you will ever face. You are taking the courage to stand up and say "No more! I have suffered enough!" Now that you are aware of the stranglehold your SDBs have on you, you are in a greater position of power to do something about it, to stand up and take action, releasing yourself from the shackles of pain and duress that have plagued your life.

Awareness leads to a stronger desire to stop your destructive SDBs and start living a life of freedom and higher mastery of self. Your commitment to recovery is the first step. There are no half measures. You must prepare to dig in so you can dig yourself up and out of the hole you have been living in. You are going to war with the darkest parts of yourself.

I urge you not to surrender, no matter how many times you have to try. Recovery from this illness is the path to real freedom, and the only road that will lead you to the truth. Once you are ready to face your deepest wounds, you have set the stage to make way for lasting, permanent changes in your life.

To release yourself from the power of negative self-behavior, first select options and thoughts that lead you away from choosing the same negative patterns over and over again. SDBs can only grow stronger if you continue to feed into the behavior through acting out the same set of old behaviors again and again.

You have to remember that every action you take, before it becomes an action, is first created as a thought, and that every thought leads to a choice, and that choice leads to an action, which produces a result.

Now is the moment of truth to turn around and stop running. There are choices to make here, and the choices you make will ultimately determine the course of your fate.

Action Workshop: The Master of Destroying Obstacles

Do you have any addictions that serve as a means of coping with your reality? If so, what rewards do you receive from the compulsive behavior of feeding these addictions? Write down your current addiction, and the advantages and disadvantages it provides you.

Do you procrastinate? When do you procrastinate? In what ways do you procrastinate? How has procrastinating been holding you back and causing you to fail? Now, write down three techniques that you are going to try to replace procrastination.

Is perfectionism a problem for you? If you aren't sure, take the time to read some literature on the subject and think about ways in which you might be a perfectionist. Now, how has perfectionism worked to your advantage? Your disadvantage?

Do you have a strong, supportive alliance of friends/family? If so, whom do you trust the most for advice within this group? What character traits does that person have that you admire?

What are some of your deepest fears? How have these fears blocked you from reaching your true potential? How will you deal with these fears from now on?

Write down your ideas and create a plan to help you face your fears, deal with them head on, and open up the channels of opportunity and advancement.

Section II: The Master of Time Investment

"Once you have mastered time, you will understand how true it is that most people overestimate what they can accomplish in a year - and underestimate what they can achieve in a decade!"

— Tony Robbins

The Value of Time

"Someone is sitting in the shade today because someone planted a tree a long time ago."

— Warren Buffet

Are you struggling to get work done? Is there not enough time in the day to get your critical tasks finished? Do you know what those critical tasks are? Would you like to implement simple strategies to help you do less and have more time to spend with people you love doing the activities you enjoy?

How, where, and with whom we spend our time reflects the value we place on our lives. When you value the time you're given, you're making use of the greatest resource at your disposal.

Effective time investment is about making good choices to efficiently utilize the time you have so you can increase the value of your living standards and quality of life. Knowing what's most valuable to you and properly allocating your time to each vital area of your life is necessary for progressive personal development.

You don't have all the time in the world to do everything, but you do have enough time to invest in the things that matter.

People always say they have no time.

I disagree.

I think we have enough time for anything we want to do. The key is to invest the time into an area of interest that will increase the value and quality of your life.

Making a commitment to master the time you have will enable you to build a level of excellence that connects you to a vigorous lifestyle. When you apply your daily activities, tasks, and work to meeting your goals and expectations, you gain control of yourself.

Managing your time is a massive challenge, and when your day is filled up with tasks, to-do-lists, meetings, projects, and SM/email messages that come in regularly, distributing the limited time you have becomes critical.

In this section of *The Discipline of Masters*, I will teach you how to:

- Create a time-wealthy balance
- Focus on doing things that matter and get results
- Build superior performance activities and time-management techniques
- Blow up your level of productivity with the power of delegating
- Manage your team of winners

The Challenge of Time Management

Our lives are full of distractions these days, but it is not worse than it used to be; we just have more choices of what to distract ourselves with. You see, the problem isn't that you get distracted easily. The issue lies in the fact that you have not really learned to govern your time effectively.

Mastering your time is easy. It is mastering yourself that is the real struggle. But by focusing on the minutes of your time, you can be more efficient, productive, and get the same amount of work done in a day.

Personally, I believe the person who is in control of their time is way ahead of the game. Remember three very important things about time investment.

1. There are twenty-four hours in a day. You have to sleep for at least six hours. This gives you sixteen–eighteen hours to spend for work, play, or relaxation.
2. You don't have to do everything. Delegating is a very powerful tool.
3. Knowing what is important to you will help you value your time.

By the time you finish this part of the book, you will have the basic strategies and develop the know-how to double output while doubling up on your free time. Keep your focus on the minutes, and the hours will take care of themselves.

Burning Your Greatest Asset

The most formidable obstacle that stands between you and your dreams is the efficient and effective use of time, a limited and irreplaceable resource. Time management, the ability to apply your time efficiently and in a manner that reflects the importance of your life, is the personal navigation system for ongoing improvement and personal success.

You will determine the tasks and steps necessary to keep your life moving forward on a steady track by adopting a set of time-based habits that build and support the key areas of your life. In order to become an effective time-investment manager, you must determine the areas of greatest importance and develop a plan of action that measurably structures a solid foundation for building the dreams of your future.

An investment of time means putting your greatest and most valuable resource to good use. To spend your life in a way that is both useful and efficient, put your time into the things that will produce the exact results you want. As soon as you determine the life you desire, one in line with your core personal values, your mind will automatically seek ways to make it happen for you.

Time management is a powerful skill that, once mastered and applied to achieving a state of excellence, links all the vital areas of life together.

Everything is connected in terms of creating goals for yourself, having a specific great purpose, and applying quality time to the work and effort that generates results. Investing your time wisely opens closed doors. Wasting time and taking for granted the time you have been given keeps those doors closed.

When you invest your time in work or an activity that has great personal value, you want to get something in return. The time and effort you invest now will pay back huge dividends someday. Investing your time consciously, and with a specific plan, is making the greatest investment ever…it is an investment in yourself!

If you want to succeed and go further than you ever dreamed possible, you will have to manage yourself in a way that focuses on the constant and never-ending improvement of a set of time-based principles. This is determining the best time of day you can put your time to work for you.

It is planning, on a daily basis, exactly what you're going to do with the time you have. The question you need to ask yourself is this: "What matters most to me, and how can I make the most out of my life with the time I have?"

Let's say, for instance, that I gave you twenty dollars and told you that you could do anything you wanted with it. What would you do? Now, I know you might be thinking that twenty dollars doesn't go far these days. But that's only if you think of it as twenty dollars. Now, what if I told you to keep this money until next week without spending it? If you do, I'll double it and give you forty dollars.

What would you do with it now? What if I continued to double your money every week for as long as you held on to it? Would you spend it or save it? You know that if you spend it, it's gone forever, and you will get something worth the same amount or less than the twenty dollars. It would be gone, and that is it. If you held on to it, however, and your money was doubling every week, imagine how far this money would go after just one year.

Now, replace the twenty dollars with one hour of time. Imagine now that for every hard-earned hour you invested in the success of your life, you were rewarded with ten hours of leisure time to spend in any way you like. Would you be interested? Would you find the time to contribute to building the life you want?

"Time = life; therefore, waste your time and waste of your life, or master your time and master your life."

— Alan Lakein

As you can see, whether or not we are investing time or money, both are precious resources. If these resources are invested and managed properly, the rate of return received over an extended period of time is exponential.

Many people spend their time the same way they spend their money—throwing it away on luxuries that eat up cash fast, like over-priced lattes, snacks, cigarettes, soda, or anything else that provides us with an instant sense of satisfaction.

The reward is in the instant gratification we feel. The loss comes later when we need money and find ourselves with empty pockets.

If you had money to invest, would you throw it down on a bad investment? Now, replace the word money with time and ask yourself the same question. How much time do you waste every hour, day, week, and year on bad time investments? Are you watching old TV reruns, gossiping, or surfing the 'net, endlessly looking for new ways to be entertained? This is how you waste both your time and life.

Time isn't free and it isn't expendable. It is limited, and each of us has only a certain amount of it. Some people have less time than others to spend. Others have more time than they know what to do with. The basic fact is that each of us has 60 minutes in an hour, 24 hours a day, 365 days a year.

This is non-negotiable and will never change. What truly matters is how and where you invest the time you do have. It is worth more to you than the price of gold; it is your life, and to waste your time is to waste everything you value.

The key is to invest your time now so that you can be free later. Do first the things that matter most and reap the rewards later. Once you have invested your time for that day or week, you have all the time in the world for those other activities that demand your attention.

Once you have invested your time and spent it working toward your goals, then put aside the time you need for movie watching, game playing, or just sitting in stillness. How you spend it is up to you, because when the future shows up years later, the investment you made will be obvious. Will you be doing the same old thing, wishing your life were different? Or will you be living the life you visualized because you invested the time necessary to get to where you wanted to go?

There is no pending guilt when you know that you have put your time toward something that's working to build your life, to make it better through improving the quality of your living conditions. Make a conscious choice to invest your time in working on who you want to be and where you want to be.

Invest your time in today so you can live your dreams tomorrow. If we are to succeed, it is imperative to know what's important; we must figure out our highest priorities and invest in them.

Time investment has a concrete plan. There is a goal with key target areas, and each target area requires a strong investment of focused concentration in order to work. That is why your priorities need to be set and established before you commit your time and resources to a special project or activity.

You have to know precisely what it is you want. Once you do, you can then work it in to your time-management plan and decide how much time is allocated to each specific area so it can succeed.

A Time-Wealthy Balance

"One cannot manage too many affairs: like pumpkins in the water, one pops up while you try to hold down the other."

— Chinese Proverb

Creating balance within the boundaries of four key areas is of vital importance to building a solid, well-balanced lifestyle. By making time for each of the following areas, you will create a powerful source of positive energy.

Family/Friendships/Relationships

Developing relationships with friends and family is a wealthy investment. Making time for the people that share our lives is what builds a solid foundation of love, happiness, and sense of well-being. It is through building relationships with friends, family, coworkers, the community, and mentors that we define who we are.

The people that share and experience life with us have the most to offer. Relationships you invest in and make time for will expand and grow over the years, forming an unbreakable bond between you and the people with you on this journey.

You can build these relationships in a variety of ways:

- Taking a "family day"—take the children on a day/weekend trip
- Staying in touch with people through social networking
- Writing a letter to someone you care about
- Sending birthday cards to distant relatives and good friends
- Encouraging your family to discuss problems and issues

- Discussing the importance of values with family and friends.

Career/Education/Professional Development

When we're not spending time with family, friends, or others, we can focus on a career and doing work we love. If you are not doing work that you love and are just showing up to get a paycheck, you are wasting your time and your employer's. The whole point to structuring our time is to create the time for spending it on things we care about.

It is the work in life that defines our skills and level of professionalism. At least 30 percent of your time invested should go into building, maintaining, and mastering a profession or field of work.

Through this pathway, new doors will open and opportunities will be created; it is through the industry of work that new skills are defined and mastered. A commitment to your professional field boosts income, develops aptitude and skill, and solidifies confidence in your ability to manage and procure a lifetime of employment.

You can support and develop your professional career in a variety of ways:

- Subscribing to or buying online educational courses (for more information, check out UniversalClass.com/Teachable/Udemy)
- Completing a degree or pursuing a master's course
- Joining a professional developmental seminar
- Reading books on business related to your field, and committing to and expanding your efforts to know everything there is to know about the object of your pursuits

- Doing the best work that you can even if the job you're in right now isn't what you want to continue doing

Hobbies/Creative Activities

This is perhaps the most overlooked area when it comes to time investment, especially for people with already heavy, busy schedules; the time for relaxing or engaging in a creative hobby is left to the end. It is usually what we do when there is time left over at the end of the week.

Instead of making time for a hobby or other form of relaxation, we do it when everything else is finished. In fact, I have heard many people say that they'd pick up where they left off with a sport or an activity that was once an area of deep interest—when they have time.

The reality is, however, that if we don't make time for those things that are fulfilling and bring joy to a hectic cycle of life, we never get around to doing anything. It ends up on the back burner, until eventually the flames go out. In the race to get life's urgencies finished up day after day, the things that make us feel good are left behind to be picked up another day. This day rarely comes.

I have met people who have given up on writing, exercise, painting, making music, and even meditation because they couldn't find the time anymore. It is true that as life progresses, responsibilities for many people increase to the point where they are maxed out at the end of the week.

If that's true for you, to fix it here is a basic rule: don't just find the time for the things that matter; you must make the time and schedule it around your priorities.

Something as simple as sitting down for thirty minutes a night to engage in something you love to do will add enormous value to the day and your life overall. Make the time for the things that are yours.

Of course, developing relationships, building careers, and taking care of family are of great importance, as is working on ridding yourself of stress, taking time to breathe, and getting focused on something that is for you.

- Write that book you've been talking about for the past decade.
- Take up painting, model building, building furniture, or drawing.
- Learn to play an instrument.
- Start up a collection of something you feel a passion for.

You don't have to do everything; you can focus on one small part of learning what you have always wanted to try. For example, if you decide to start playing the piano, instead of thinking about how it will take you years to learn, just focus on learning one new key a week.

Focus on that key for the week before moving on. You can use this mini-strategy for just about everything. Break the task own into a small goal.

Exercise, Sports, and Eating Right

You have to make time for your health. I know, in the busy-ness of our busy lives, exercise is something that we do when we have time for it. We treat it as a side hobby that we only do when we feel like. But your body is getting older. People who make exercise a habit and practice this habit for thirty minutes a day live longer and enjoy a healthier lifestyle. This includes making the time for eating well.

For example, I exercise in the morning first thing within ten minutes of waking up. I drink a glass of fruit juice, and then start working out at home with a few weights and a medicine ball.

"I don't have time to get the gym" is a common excuse we feed ourselves. Set yourself up at home with a few things. I bought a 5 kg medicine ball six months ago and I haven't been to the gym since then, and I am actually in better shape.

Spend time each week investing in your body and mind. You can:

1. Buy some home workout equipment such as free weights, a medicine ball, or ab cruncher. You don't need much space and there are no membership fees.

2. Prepare your meals the night before. Taking time out at the end of the day can save you time and stop you from dashing to the fast food restaurant.

Spiritual and Mental Health Development

How much time do you invest in improving and developing your spiritual and mental development? Do you read self-help books? Attend motivational seminars or counseling sessions? You're reading this book, and that is a great way to flex your mental muscles for growth and find new ways to improve yourself.

Regardless of how successful or fulfilled we might be in the first three areas, if you neglect to make time for cleaning your mental health department, you run the risk of growing negative, bitter, and depressed.

People that fail to "clean" their minds of useless thoughts build up a collection of old, worn-out ideas and ideals. To improve, we must improvise; to develop and make forward progress, we must contribute to a system of never-ending self-improvement.

- Put aside twenty minutes a day for meditation or mental cleansing.
- Read books by Hal Urban, Pema Chodron, Stephen Covey, the Dalai Lama, M. Scott Peck, James Allen, Anthony Robbins, and Napoleon Hill.
- Erase your impure thoughts with positive quotes or affirmations.
- Help another person succeed.
- Be honest with yourself and others, practice integrity, and—above all—be kind.
- Make a list of character traits you value and focus on integrating these values into your life.

Financial Investment and Retirement

A good, solid financial portfolio will someday provide you with the freedom to do whatever you want. The old "Time is money" adage has never been truer when it comes to setting up the future for financial success. In fact, failing to have a financial plan of any kind is planning to fail big time, and time is exactly what you will lose.

Instead of possibly retiring early at fifty-five or sixty, you could end up working well into your seventies or, even worse, retire broke, with all the time in the world but no money to do anything with the time you have. At the very least, you should be putting away 10 percent of everything you earn monthly, without exception.

You don't have to be a financial wizard or have a doctorate in economics to work out a financial plan. You can find plenty of easy-to-follow books that can be read in just a few hours. The time you take to read these books and apply their ideas and techniques could save you years.

I would recommend Think and Grow Rich by Napoleon Hill and The Automatic Millionaire by David Bach. The information and advice in these books is relatively simple to follow and will set you on the path to building a life instead of just working for one.

In the end, we all want more time to do the things that matter most, and if you have the cash to support your dreams, then time really is on your side. To get your financial house in order, follow these few tips:

- Put aside 10–15 percent of your salary into a separate savings account or mutual fund
- Cut down on buying the stuff you don't need
- Create a financial plan for every year
- Only have one credit card
- Concentrate on eliminating personal debt, and start a home-based internet business

Priority Investment Planning

"How different our lives are when we really know what is deeply important to us, and keeping that picture in mind, we manage ourselves each day to be and to do what really matters most."

— Stephen Covey

The first step to mastering time investment so you can effectively master the minutes of your day is through a system I call priority investment planning (PIP). This technique is used for establishing your priorities in life, so you can concentrate on the important matters.

You have to know what is most valuable to you so that you don't get caught up in contributing to those activities and distractions that have little or no value.

Unfortunately, most people are not in control of their time, and because of this, they are not in control of their lives. Are you continuously struggling for more time to spend with your family? Is someone dictating to you how and when to do things? Is too much of your time spent pleasing others? Do you constantly complain about having no time, only to spend it wrapped up in trivial matters and empty tasks?

If so, it is important to understand that you are not in control of your life until you learn to be in control of yourself—that is, learn self-management so you're utilizing your most precious resource: time! PIP puts you in control of your life.

Most people never figure out their priorities, and so they spend all their time chasing unimportant, non-urgent matters and responding to the never-ending needs and demands of others.

The Golden Egg of Time Investment

Prioritizing your tasks and goals is the process of taking those things that matter most—that is, the goals and aims that contribute to your true values and the creation of a vision you have for the rest of your life.

Once you have those goals and aims, you will create a plan to carry out the plan. That is, through priority time investment, you will decide what goals are most important and require daily intense concentration to succeed. In other words, you are putting what matters most first.

In Stephen Covey's wonderful book, The 7 habits of Highly Effective People, he tells us that to be most effective in the area of time management, we must "organize and execute around priorities." This is exactly what we're going to do: determine the most important things in your life and build the rest of your world around those high-level activities.

Time Control = Action Management

Organizing your priorities and putting into order of importance the things that matter most is a powerful organizational skill. Clarifying and defining goals and projects is one thing but is only the beginning.

A goal without immediate follow-up action is just words on paper. In order to be truly effective, you have to know the actions you're going to take and why you're taking them. Having said this, it isn't enough to just schedule our priorities and hope it all works out in the end. You have to take proactive measures to control your actions in relation to those priorities.

In order to be truly effective and make a recognizable difference in your life, you have to organize your busy schedule around these priorities. This means that, no matter how many things you have on the go today or this week, determine the actions you must take to complete the work you want to achieve.

Know your tasks for the day and for your week. If you fail to do this, the things that matter most will be buried under heaps of other "little" things, or the stuff that matters least. If you can manage your actions—that is, work on those activities, tasks, and projects that deliver high value—you automatically begin to define the skills necessary for mastering your time. It really is that simple.

When I look around at the actions people take, I can see the difference in people that are working because they have to and those with a deeper purpose. The latter know why they're busy and what they have to do to achieve goals and meet demands.

Many people I notice keep busy to avoid falling into lethargy, or to avoid getting scolded by a supervisor that wants to see them looking busy. It is the select few, however, with actions that are directed toward a specific purpose that will accomplish their greatest dreams.

Make an Action List

Now, referring again to the list of goals you created, are the actions you partake in every week contributing to meeting your desired accomplishments? If so, that is great. Continue to work at it, monitor and review your progress regularly, and stay focused on what matters.

If your actions are not yet in line with your dreams, it's time to stop what you're doing. I would suggest right here that you take a look at what you're doing and ask if it's contributing to your future.

Are you just killing time for the sake of pleasing others? Begin to question your reasons for doing things—your job, your activities, your habits—and shift the things that need to be changed.

Take the time now to complete this short exercise. Choose something you've been meaning to start but just haven't found the time. Is your house a mess? Does your desktop need to have a good cleaning? Is there a project that's been on your to-do list for the past five years?

Whatever it may be, choose something right now to work on. Now, for the next twenty minutes, I want you to do some form of action on that activity. You can set a timer if you want to, but for the next twenty minutes you're going to do something that contributes toward the progress of this project, no matter how big or small it is.

If you've been trying to start a book for the past year, write the first page (or the last). Make a chapter list. Do anything. Don't even think too long or hard about what you're going to do. Just do something. Make your next action count.

After twenty minutes have passed, stop if you can and observe how you feel. Do you feel excited and motivated to continue, or like a great pressure valve has been released and now, instead of putting off this job or task, you know it's possible to do it if you take some action?

Even if it's something that will take you months or years to complete, taking that first step gives you momentum. Instead of wasting time thinking about doing it, you can start to do it whenever you want.

Organizing Things That Matter

What's most important to you now? Is it raising a family? Winning an election or giving a public speech? Starting your own company? Getting into the best physical shape possible? Volunteering your services? Learning a new language?

Upgrading your education so you can get a better job that's more in line with your true talents? Reading a series of books on how to do something?

Changing your job to another profession more in line with your purpose for living? Building the house of your dreams? Saving money for your house of dreams? What makes you feel enthusiastic and motivated? Where is your passion the strongest? Are your daily activities in line with your character values? When do you feel the most enthusiastic and energetic?

Know what you feel passionate about and you will find time for it. It's the people without a purpose that kill time, and in actuality, they are killing themselves. Time is the air we breathe; when you're out of time, you're out of life. To be truly effective in your family, career and business, finance, and self-development, your priorities within each of these areas must be first!

Organizing your priorities and knowing specifically what they are is the formula for mastering time investment. It's not about controlling all the little stuff or attempting to keep busy just so you look productive. It is concentrating and dedicating your time to a particular target.

You focus on your highest ambitions and do what has to be done to achieve victory within the areas that have your passion at heart. Concentrate on the activities, people, and things that will have a massive impact on the way of life you're striving for.

So, how do you know what your priority is for this week, or even for today? Up to this point everything you were doing probably felt like a priority-one situation. Dealing with everything as it's thrown at you has become an unconscious habit. It's in our nature to respond with a sudden reaction whenever a crisis occurs, or we're called to the line of duty.

We should try to stop reacting to every little event as if we need to fix it. Maybe you do and maybe you don't. The point is learning to choose what needs to be done by you and what can be done by someone else. As I learned to adjust my schedule around my priorities, I stopped treading down the path of least resistance. Learning I didn't have to try to please everyone, I knew when to say no.

The key is to select and focus on those master areas of your life that will contribute to the overall progress, growth, and quality of your life. The master areas I spend the most time on contribute in some small way to designing the world I will live in in five, ten, or twenty years. In other words, I focus on the activities that are in a direct relationship with my master goals and contribute to the achievement of those goals.

It's easy to know where your priorities are: just take a look at the things that add the greatest value to your life and you'll have an instant understanding of what you're supposed to do with your limited time resources. The actions I engage in are constructive and positive life-building activities.

> *"If you want to make good use of your time, you've got to know what's most important and then give it all you've got."*
>
> **— Lee Iacocca**

Recognizing the priority thoughts, words, and actions that govern your life is a way of valuing yourself. Remember that if you are not fixated on a goal or high-end priority tasks, you're probably fixated on something else; this is a distraction that pulls you off course and steers you in the wrong direction. This is where people lose time.

When I'm distracted or get pulled into something else, it takes me hours or even days before I get back to what I was doing initially. Remember that your high-level priority workload grows out of your desires. The subconscious knows what it wants and will help you prioritize to get it.

When you schedule your daily, weekly, and monthly priorities, keep these important factors in mind:

- Be very clear and exact about what you want to achieve
- Prioritize those activities that take you closer to your desired accomplishments. Give them first place on your priority list
- Work your schedule to fit around your priorities
- Focus on life design, not life crises
- Learn to say no to "urgent" matters that don't matter
- Delegate tasks to other people when needed
- Be flexible in your scheduling
- Reward yourself vigorously when you complete a goal or priority
- Enjoy yourself—creating your destiny is fun
- Ensure your priorities reflect your personal values—they are a statement of what you want the most.

When you do the things that matter most, even when you don't want to do them but you schedule them anyways, you are practicing a form of self-management. You do what needs to be done, even when you don't feel like doing it. This is the foundation for developing self-discipline and diligence in everything you do.

Organizing priorities is one of the master keys to time investment. In order to invest your time in something that will bring you a good return, you have to know what you're investing in; you must consciously choose the areas you will allocate your time to.

Time Management Performance Techniques

> *"One cannot manage too many affairs: like pumpkins in the water, one pops up while you try to hold down the other."*
>
> **— Chinese Proverb**

The 168 technique is a simple idea that works extremely well if you're focusing on balancing your time to become more efficient, or if you're just looking to free up some extra time so you can relax more.

168 Time-Blocking Technique

How it works is simple: one block equals an hour. There are 168 blocks, or units, in a week. With 168 blocks of time, you are going to sleep, eat, work, and prioritize your activities to manage your time and make the best use of your minutes. As you think about planning for this week or next, you're going to assign blocks of time to each activity.

Try not to spread your time too thin and remember that the purpose of this technique is to create a wealthy, healthy balance of your most precious resource so you can live as an efficient, healthy, and happy person.

How It Works

We are each given 168 blocks a week. Assuming you sleep 7 hours a night, you now have 121 hours to divide up within your week. If you work from 9:00 to 5:30, you now have 78 hours/blocks. Now here's where it gets interesting. If you have already slept and worked a full week, there are still 78 hours remaining, give or take a few depending on circumstances. As you can see from this, there is enough time left over for you to do the things you want to do.

One of the reasons this technique is so effective is because, when you treat every hour as a tangible something you can envision in the form of a unit or block, your time has value. Instead of just using time or spending it, we're now in a position to manage ourselves more effectively.

Take a look at your week and see how you're going to invest in it. What would you do if each unit of your time was worth $100,000? Would you treat each hour differently? If the time in your life had the same value as cash in your pocket, wouldn't you spend it more carefully?

Of course, you still don't know what's going to happen to you this week, whom you're going to meet, or what circumstances will fall your way. This system is very flexible and allows you to plan for the unexpected. Perhaps your boss asks you to stay late at the office every night this week, and instead of the usual seven or eight hours of sleep, you decide to sleep in two days. That's fine.

This technique requires some juggling around as you move your time blocks into position. I make changes almost daily to my time-blocking schedule, but it's a lot of fun. By doing this, you know where you're spending your time. If you must increase your time blocks for one area, such as in your job or if something suddenly comes up, you simply take a block from one area and put it in another.

This is where your priorities come in. If at all possible, don't steal time from these areas. If you do this right, you still have lots of time to play with. One of the reasons we fail to use time efficiently isn't because we don't have enough of it, but because we don't know what to do with the time we do have.

Start by creating your 168 time-blocking plans for the week. Remember to stick to your priorities and allocate enough time for fun and games. Most time schedules people make for themselves are very tight, sometimes right down to the last hour. This can be hectic if everything doesn't go according to plan, and it very rarely does.

I leave at least five blocks of time in reserve for flexibility, in case of little emergencies or if I want to spend an extra hour or two with the kids. Tuck these hours away at the bottom of the page. If the end of the week is near and you don't foresee any unexpected events, take them and have fun.

The Pomodoro Technique

This is a strategy designed to get you to take immediate action in twenty-five-minute increments. How it works is simple. You can download the app or set your timer for twenty-five minutes. Then, you work for twenty-five minutes on one project. You don't deviate or do something else. You stay fixed on the one activity. After twenty-five minutes, take a five-minute break. Then, go again.

This is great for breaking procrastination and getting started on a project you have been putting off. By tackling something in short chunks, we can deal with it without feeling overwhelmed.

- Download the Tomato Timer app
- Set the timer for twenty-five min
- Take a five min break
- Start session two
- Repeat as many times as you can

Declutter Your Stuff

You may not think about it but living in a space surrounded by clutter is robbing you of your time. Do you ever spend time looking for something you need right at that moment? I know I have, and if my workspace had been in better order, I would have saved a lot of time.

Our clutter not only keeps us from staying focused, but it is a distraction. Distractions waste time. You can significantly reduce your clutter by spending just ten minutes a day cleaning up a part of your house or committing to getting rid of one thing a day.

Think about what your room, desk, or office would look like if it were reduced to a minimalist state. Can you imagine how relaxed you would feel? How much more productive you would be? How much time you could save by staying focused instead of being pulled away by the clutter getting in your way?

You don't have to totally minimize your environment, but if you are drowning in clutter, both in your physical and digital environment, it could be time to do something about it.

Action Steps: Get Decluttered

Set aside a block of time for decluttering. This can be fifteen minutes, thirty minutes, or a block of one hour.

Decide what you are decluttering: Is it your closet? Kitchen? Desktop?

Once you start to declutter something, stay focused on that one area until you are finished. If you start with that place under your bed, even if it takes you three days of short increments to get it done, stick with it. When done, move on to the next.

Make a clear decision on everything you touch. You either keep it or toss it. If you keep it, put it where it belongs. If you can't decide right now whether you need it or not, put it in a box and leave it there with the other undecided items.

Then, after three months, if you still haven't touched it, toss it or sell it. Chances are you are just holding on to it for fear of letting go.

Schedule a Fifteen-minute Weekly Planning Session

Start each new week with fifteen minutes of goal-planning time. During this session with yourself, write a list of priority goals and tasks for that week. Then, break down those tasks into manageable steps. Making a weekly schedule or priority task list focuses your concentration on the things that matter most. Without this, like a ship with a broken rudder, you'll soon find yourself veering off course.

To make the most effective use of your time each and every day, set aside fifteen minutes at the beginning of each week to make your weekly schedule. Once your goals for that week have been determined, put them in order of importance and tackle them one by one. Write down the steps you have to do for each goal and keep your plan visible at all times, in a place you have easy access to.

As the weeks and months go by, you'll be amazed at the progress you're making. Every week should have a priority goals list, and your first priority is to make a schedule for your master priorities. At the end of the week, if there are any tasks that didn't get finished, move them over to the following week and continue to do so until they get done

Balance Your Activities

Balance in life is everything. To live up to your own expectations and personal values, you need a true balance in the vital areas of your life. Don't just commit to one area of your life and spend eighteen hours a day focused on this one thing. While doing so guarantees you will become a master at this one thing, the other parts of your life will fall apart if neglected.

If you spend day and night working in the office but neglect to build a strong relationship with your wife and children, you won't be truly successful in your efforts. Your family will grow apart, and you might be faced with a broken home, losing everything you were working for.

If you forget to make improvements on your character development every now and then, you'll eventually build up a deep emptiness inside through character deprivation. You can be totally successful in one or two areas of your life but a complete failure in others.

The most successful people are those that dedicate time to the various parts of living. Commit your time to each vital area, even if it's only a short amount of time, and you'll feel fulfilled and satisfied. Working sixteen hours a day and rushing home to eat and sleep isn't exactly a well-balanced lifestyle. You can do it for a while, but if this continues for an extended period of time, your balance scales will tip over.

In other words, your efforts will result in misery and burnout. Balancing the importance of your life takes time and practice. It is a skill that becomes easier the more effort you put into it.

Know what matters and contribute a piece of each day or week to a healthy way of living. Don't work too much, and don't play too much. But do both as much as possible.

Organize Your Systems

Organization plays an important role in saving and investing time. Nothing defeats an organized individual with a clean desk who has every paper put away into neat files. You can build fast, efficient systems for everything you do, even the housework. I can't stress enough the importance of utilizing this powerful skill to save time and money.

To organize your paperwork, make files for things you want to keep. The trick is simple: move everything only once! That is, if you have moved the same piece of paper around six times, it's obviously not in the right place. Organization is about putting things in the right place so when the time comes for you to use that material, it's in your hands within seconds.

You know where it is and you don't spend minutes, hours, or weeks looking for it. If you lose something valuable, you have to replace it if it's lost. How much time have you spent looking for things that could have been filed away in their proper places?

Now, try these ideas for getting organized and maintaining that organization.

1. Make files for everything. Important papers, especially your goals and working statement, need a place you can access easily and quickly. If you spend more than twenty seconds looking for something, it's in the wrong place.

2. Touch it only once. Don't shift a pile of papers from one desk to another. You will only end up shifting them again. Move it once and remember where it is.

3. Practice getting organized. This is a skill that improves over time. The more you do it, the more efficient you become at it, and you save thousands of hours in the long run.

4. Put everything back when you're finished. One of my habits is to use something and leave it someplace else. This means that the next time I want to use it, I have to spend time looking for it, or somebody else does. It only takes a second to return what you used.

The Power of Delegating

> *"Until we can manage time, we can manage nothing else."*
>
> **— Peter F. Drucker**

What would you do if your biggest dreams and lifelong goals required some special skills that you didn't have? What if you needed some high-level technical training or years of schooling in order to accomplish the things you really wanted to do?

What if you had very limited time to get that training? How would you deal with a project that required the trade, skills, and ideas of a thousand individual minds?

The answer to these questions brings us to the power of delegating, the fastest and most efficient way to increase efficiency and save you years, if not decades, of time. This is the secret behind the success of thousands of people that have accelerated their growth and development at a phenomenal rate, combining the skills, knowledge, and work of the many in order to succeed and achieve the impossible within a limited timeframe.

If you take a look at any successful business entrepreneur, president, or world-class, high-level achiever, you will see the work of hundreds or thousands of people involved in the success of this individual. These successful people found the people that had the skills, information, talents, and knowledge they didn't have and hired them.

This goes for anything that requires dozens of individual skills working together for similar goals. The success of an individual, company, city, or country is realized by the combined effort of the many. Each of us has the same amount of time every day, and you can only accomplish so much as one individual.

When people combine their efforts and skills and dedicate these talents to a specific purpose, their productivity and efficiency increase exponentially. If two people working together can do double the work in the same amount of time, imagine what a hundred or a thousand people can do if given a specific job and priorities to fulfill. Cities and empires are created this way. Families are created this way. The success of global companies and world change is created this way.

We all have the same amount of time every day: twenty-four hours. This is constant, non-negotiable, and will never change. We have just twenty-four hours in which to sleep, eat, work, and enjoy recreational activities. Maybe you think this isn't enough time. Some days it can feel this way. You have loads of housework to do, a report due by the end of the week, and a task list that grows daily.

These are obstacles everyone faces as we struggle with deadlines and hectic schedules, and only have twenty-four hours to do it all in. The clock is racing, and you can't catch up to it.

What if I were to tell you that you could expand your time and resources? What if, instead of the usual twenty-four hours a day, you were given thirty-two hours a day? Would it make a difference in the quality of your life? Could you get everything done? Would it be more time you could spend with friends or family? Would you be able to relax, knowing that the work needed to get the job done is in more capable hands than just your own?

Well, through delegating work to other people, you can increase the time you have available for other things. It is a strategy used by businesses, entrepreneurs, and successful people all over the world, all of whom have the same time available to them as you and me, yet they achieve so much more in a day than most people can get done in a year.

The reason for this is simple: They delegate the tasks that others can do, and they do the tasks that only they can do.

It is through this method that you exponentially increase your time. You pass the work on to people that possess the proper skills and qualifications to achieve the goals you desire. Movie makers, writers, corporate CEOs, musicians, and even performers—everyone benefits from delegated work. They understand the importance and significance of delegating their visions and dreams to people with similar interests.

It doesn't matter what your dream is, how big it is, or how impossible it might seem. It is only impossible if you try to do it alone. People that go about it alone accomplish very little. They become masters of nothing because they are too busy trying to master everything.

"I Can Do It All!"

Delegating sometimes costs money, and other times it doesn't. You don't have to fork over huge amounts of cash to get something done. Not all of us can afford a personal secretary or a private team of advanced professionals working around the clock.

However, when faced with a situation where they don't have the time, resources, or proper skills to get a job done, those with mega success outsource the work instead of spending hundreds of hours researching how to do it. The golden rule of delegating is to do what you can and delegate the rest.

There are people that hate to delegate any kind of workload. They don't like trusting others to do the work because they think and believe they can do it much better. They want to get all the credit for the job, and to show everyone else that they did it and can do anything on their own.

People operating from this position are rarely willing to listen to the advice of others that could add new input or take a project in a new direction. They often do the one thing that places them at the bottom of the list: they fail to learn. Furthermore, they fail to give others the opportunity to express their own talents and creativity. You might eventually get all the credit, but you won't have anyone to share it with if you try to do it all.

Through delegating necessary work, you're increasing the productivity and efficiency of projects. If you're able to convince others that your vision is a real winner, you could develop a powerful support system of professionals willing to lend you their invaluable ideas and input.

If you don't find a way to delegate at least a small portion of your workload, thereby adding more time to your days, you'll end up working longer hours, your stress will increase dramatically, and—eventually—you won't be working at all.

If you try to make it on your own, you'll be a tortoise racing against lions. Success in work or with projects is accomplished much faster and easier through the combined efforts of a group of individuals sharing a similar vision and working toward a definite purpose.

Time really is money, and if you consider this when delegating, remember that for every hour you save through delegating, you could be doubling your income, doubling your private time spent at home, or kicking up your feet on a beach in Bali, while those at home are doing the work that you organized.

If you follow the steps for successful delegating listed in the section below, you will reap some powerful rewards from distributing work to others.

It pays to delegate because it...

- Is the fastest way to boost your efficiency and productivity
- Expands your valuable resources
- Provides you with more time to focus on personal goals
- Significantly reduces mistakes and increases damage control abilities
- Reduces personal workloads and stress
- Provides others with the opportunity to boost their confidence and increase their personal skill levels
- Reduces pressure to do it all by yourself and helps increase your trust in others

Whether you're a company CEO or a homemaker, delegating gives you more time and energy to do the things you want to do.

The Ten Pillars of Delegating

> "Time is the coin of your life. It is the only coin you have, and only you can determine how it will be spent. Be careful lest you let other people spend it for you."
>
> — Carl Sandburg

These ten delegating steps to success are utilized by successful managers, organizations, corporations, and private individuals to meet workplace demands in the everyday world.

Clearly share your vision with everyone involved.

Clearly explain the goals, objectives, and expected outcomes to everyone involved in the work. For families who share housework, at the beginning of the week, the family will hold a short meeting in which they discuss their goals for the week, as well as each person's responsibilities for the week. The chairperson—the mother or the father—delegates the work to be done.

Every morning in Japan, factory and shop workers gather together for a brief "warm-up" session before starting the workday. They discuss each other's responsibilities and the goals for that day, followed by a short stretching session.

It is important that everyone have goals and understand the important role they play in helping achieve those goals. The vision is shared by everyone, and each person involved works to bring that vision to life.

Keep an open line of communication.

When it comes to delegating work, have an open line of communication with your employees, staff, coworkers, or family members. One of the keys to success for any organization is to hold regular meetings to check everyone's progress, discuss problems people are having, and discuss some of the solutions to those problems.

A lack of communication results in heavy time and money losses. If it isn't always feasible to bring everyone together for a meeting, sending out regular email is a viable alternative.

Offer suggestions, feedback, and evaluate progress.

When you delegate work to another person, even if it is a professional with years of experience, they still require your advice and feedback on the progress of the work. If you don't give this, they could make mistakes that could have been avoided, and once again, the resources that you're trying to protect are wasted.

If you're too busy to do this, find a delegate to represent you—somebody who knows the work as well as you do and can track its progress and offer positive suggestions and feedback to everyone involved.

Make a tracking list for delegated tasks.

Always keep a list of who is doing what, what their deadlines are, and any pressing problems or concerns that people need help with. It depends on the size of the project, but if you lose track of where your work is, it will be very difficult to monitor progress and talk to the people directly involved.

Keep records of everything that has been handed out and regularly follow up with the people performing the work. Remember, though, that your work isn't done once you delegate tasks; rather, it is just beginning.

Train people when necessary.

You might have times when work or a project delegated to people requires an upgrade in their skills and knowledge. This training might be in the form of a small presentation, a seminar, on-the-job training, or a meeting to discuss the job at hand and what is involved. The scale of the work is not important. When you delegate, you are still responsible for the final outcome.

If someone makes an error because they didn't have proper training or lacked the information to do the job right, you are accountable. Mistakes and errors are going to happen no matter how well people are informed, but you can greatly reduce the damage through training people beforehand. Once again, communication plays a powerful role when delegating work.

Furthermore, an investment in upgrading people's skills is an investment in yourself. I have known employers or managers that have fired loyal, long-standing employees simply because that person's knowledge and skills were a little outdated.

Instead of taking the time and investing a little money in a valuable asset, they brought in new staff that had the proper skills but lacked familiarity with the environment and systems. These people had to be trained despite their education whereas that money could have been spent instead on the employees that just had outdated information. Whose fault is it? I think you can guess.

Once again, remember to show people what is expected of them, and then show them how to get the results you desire. Don't give up on people before they show you what they're capable of if given the chance.

Don't pass the blame. Stay accountable for your work.

When things go wrong, the first instinct for some people is to find the person responsible and give them a good scolding. Unfortunately, thousands of people lose their jobs every year due to an error made not by them, but the person they reported to.

Perhaps that person didn't have all the details or lacked the proper skills to complete the task. In any case, the responsibility for work passed out is shared by you and the delegated individual. Passing blame to another is a lose-lose situation for both parties and is something you want to avoid at all costs.

Praise good work.

Work that is worthy must be praised. I have worked for people in the past who, no matter how hard you worked, never recognized good efforts. They only acknowledged work done poorly or wrongly. It doesn't matter if the person delegated the task is getting paid for it or not; they still need to be praised.

Acknowledgement of good work feels good and boosts the confidence of all those involved; it instills in people the motivation to do even better the next time. Something as simple as praising people is good for families, business, and relationships.

Assign work to the right person.

Before you delegate work to someone or hire an outside source, first make sure that person or company is right for the job. It is your responsibility to find the right people, and making a mistake, such as passing the work on to someone that doesn't have the proper skills, could cost you a lot of money and valuable time.

For example, I wouldn't ask somebody to fix my car's engine if they couldn't identify a spark plug. Always assign work to the most capable person and provide them with as much detail as possible.

Don't overload.

Don't overload any one person with more than they can handle. This is a terrible waste of resources because if you value that person as an effective resource and a key delegate, loading them up with too much work causes them stress, and the work won't be done properly.

People that are overworked will work faster to get rid of the things on their to-do list, but the work will be sloppy and not as good as it could've been had they only had one task to accomplish.

Be professional.

I have worked with many people, and I cherish those experiences when employees were treated as part of the business: the managers provided praise and encouragement, feedback, and training for my weaker areas. This was a very professional way to keep morale high and encourage people to do the best they could.

I have worked in other professions that treated people just the opposite. Workers were considered expendable and verbally mistreated and very little encouragement was provided with regard to the quality of work done. This is unprofessional and creates a negative environment.

If you're in charge of delegating work or are the one receiving responsibility, remember that a professional attitude is something that people will always remember you for. It will also keep the good people in your company, and when you have enough good people working with or for you, the opportunities to build and create something new are increased tenfold.

Treat people with respect and admiration. Trust them to do the tasks you clearly define. These are the keys to maintaining a successful career, family environment, or business.

The Time Investor's Twenty-Three-Point Checklist

Here is a final checklist you can use to stay focused on what matters most.

1. Place priority matters first.
2. Say no to distractions. Use the Pro Focus app to build in a focused time block.
3. Prepare a daily/weekly/monthly priority action list, and then work to achieve your goals one goal at a time.
4. Focus on just one thing until done.
5. Spend ten minutes a day decluttering your home. Get rid of one thing a day through recycling or giving it away to someone who needs it.
6. Create a well-balanced lifestyle: focus on the vital areas of family and relationship matters, hobbies and interests, money management, spiritual development, learning, and professional development.
7. Invest time into the people that matter most.
8. Say no more often to the small stuff that demands your immediate attention.
9. Use a calendar. Schedule everything using the 168 time-blocking technique.
10. Be diligent about your schedule and deadlines.
11. Do not steal time from others through creating unnecessary problems.

12. Remember: time is money and having more money can buy you the time to do what you most desire to do.

13. Avoid excessive channel surfing or excessive TV watching, two of the biggest time wasters. Schedule your internet and TV time and limit the amount you consume.

14. Take the time to think things through and be mindful of the moments.

15. Invest in learning as much as you can about time and money management.

16. Practice the habit of ten-minute focused concentration. Set a timer and focus your energy into something for ten minutes.

17. Focus on the quality of your projects and not the quantity. Wake up half an hour early and get to work on your most important task.

18. Break your work into twenty-five-minute chunks.

19. Break big projects into small, incremental tasks. Work on one task until finished.

20. Monitor your time spent on a project or task. You can use the Egg Timer.

21. Delegate the work to people that can do it better and faster than you.

22. Prepare your "must-do" list every night for the next day.

23. Don't waste your time in pointless banter or complaining sessions.

Section III: The Master of Mentoring and Leadership

"In every art, beginners must start with models of those who have practiced the same art before them. And it is not only a matter of looking at the drawings, paintings, musical compositions, and poems that have been and are being created; it is a matter of being drawn into the individual work of art, of realizing that it has been made by a real human being and trying to discover the secret of its creation."

— Ruth Whitman

You, the Mentor

> *"Leaders should influence others. In such a way that it builds people up, encourages and educates them so they can duplicate this attitude in others."*
>
> **— Bob Goshen**

Mentoring is the journey of two people working together to achieve a significant goal or mission. As a mentor, your purpose for taking on this role is based largely on the needs and goals of the mentee. But for the most part, the purpose may be to work through a particular trial in life, to help someone achieve a lifelong goal, or to provide companionship and support for someone who needs it.

Here I am giving you a simple program to get started on your mentoring journey. Now, before we begin, you might think mentoring is not for you or you may not like leading people. But actually, we all do some form of mentoring in some area of our lives. If you are a parent, you want to be a role model (mentor) for your kids. If you coach sports, you are a mentor.

If you are a manager at work, you are filling the role of a mentor. Only, we disguise the word mentor with parent, teacher, or boss and, in many cases, we perform the role without asking for it. You may have thought you were given a choice to mentor or not. But that's not always the case.

Again, regardless if you are in charge of a classroom, people at work, or you just want to make a difference in someone's life by showing them the way to leading a better one, knowing how to reach people and help them on this journey is a privilege and not a duty.

So, here we are: You, The **Mentor**.

There are mentors for every area of life. You could be the person in someone's life who helps them overcome challenges and succeed. When they fall and need help getting back into the race, you could be the one to run with them toward the finish line.

If you are ready to make a difference and help others transform their lives, it is time to become a mentor. This is the road to leadership that anyone with willingness can practice.

The Need for a Mentor

Millions of people in the world today are grappling to gain control of the ongoing cycles of change occurring in their lives. We find ourselves lost in a bitter struggle against ourselves, in a growing epidemic of people who have taken up arms against the disappointment of life's false promises.

We are barely able to keep up with the ever-increasing demands surrounding us as we struggle to have more and be more when all we really want is to live more.

Too many people are lost in confusion: failed dreams; relationships that promise too much and then wither; deep feelings of discontentment, restlessness, and anxiety; and a lack of strong character values that has led to an even deeper lack of purpose in life.

People are discovering that after a life of chasing success and obtaining all the material goods they could possibly imagine, it wasn't what they really wanted in the first place.

Many of us came to the end of the road only to discover it was a dead end all along.

People are discovering that they just want to be better people, to be of service to the community and to each other, and to possess the valuable character traits that speak the truth about who they really are.

It is a revelation to discover that the map we have been following has been misleading. It has taken us down a different path than we originally intended, with a road full of lesser promises and ambiguity. Now we are like children lost in the deep woods of life without a compass and with nobody to guide us out of the darkness.

Life has become a race without a winner—a race of futility to make more money, have more time, prosper, be educated and find gainful employment, get married, raise a family, buy a home, and make it to retirement with enough to survive the remaining years of our lives. In the race to obtain more, we have become less.

Our lives are shrinking as we lose touch with who we really are and the things that really matter. The person you see in the mirror may not be the person you imagined yourself becoming.

As we move into an age of new awareness, people are becoming more conscious of their real needs. They want more than just fancy job titles, unfulfilling tasks, or designer clothes and fancy cars that promise to define their character.

People today are seeking something of greater significance, to develop a clearer sense of direction and a higher sense of self by defining who they want to be.

We are gradually awakening to the idea that hidden treasures of abundance have yet to be discovered. We want more than to survive; we want to be a part of the world, to build it, and to make a positive contribution that will have a profound impact on the lives of others.

In short, people are searching for a dream, a grander vision, a greater purpose, and—more than anything—they want help to obtain it.

> *"A leader is one who knows the way, goes the way, and shows the way."*
>
> **— John C. Maxwell**

This is where mentoring plays a dominant role in the development of our people and the world in which we live. I truly believe that a mentoring partnership with another person is the direct path to all of these things and more.

The fact is, most of the people you know—at work, your friends, or even within your own household—rarely see the real you. They see what you want them to see and depending on your role in the relationship or level of trust and honesty, people are only getting a glimpse of the real you, just enough to keep them satisfied and feel safe.

The mentoring relationship is an opportunity to take on a new role in life; it is a chance to participate in the growth and development of another person through working together to build a positive relationship. You are providing a valuable service to people so they might benefit and grow from your experiences and wisdom.

It is a journey without end, and it begins the moment you decide to make a difference through this dedication to a good cause.

Building the Mentoring Partnership

"Self-esteem is a huge piece of my work. You have to believe it's possible and believe in yourself. Because after you've decided what you want, you have to believe it's possible, and possible for you, not just for other people. Then you need to seek out models, mentors, and coaches."

—Jack Canfield

The development of a mentoring program with another person gives you the chance to have a one-on-one relationship built on trust and open honesty. The mentor and mentee discuss life on a variety of subjects, sometimes touching on very intimate matters that we would never risk discussing with even our closest friends or family.

By becoming a mentor, you are taking up an oath to support, encourage, and help others discover the magnificent qualities within themselves. Where there is a lack of purpose, you help the client realize their role in life through discovering what they were put on this Earth to do.

The question still asked by many is, "Why do I need a mentor?" First of all, nobody needs a mentor, just as it's not absolutely necessary to become a mentor. If you feel it is something that you have to do but your heart is not in it, I would recommend another course of action. If you are passionate about becoming a mentor, then your life and the lives of those you touch will grow exponentially.

Nothing compares to the way you feel when you make a positive contribution to someone else's quality of life. By helping one person, you may be helping others your mentee interacts with.

Helping People Get What They Want

Ask yourself: What does this person want the most, and how can I help them get it? This is the beginning of a great discovery. From this moment on, when you commit to helping people get what they want, you are not only giving them something, you are also pursuing your own success. It is a win-win situation.

If you want to get what you want someday, first figure out how to get it for other people. If you can do this, you will never again have to worry about the future.

The foundation for living successfully is to learn the principles of building a good life, not only for yourself but first for other people.

The mentor's purpose displaces the old way of thinking. There are people out there, people just like you, who want to pass on what they know, to build in others what they want to create in themselves. These are the people we want to discover.

One of the primary purposes for becoming a mentor is to help another become a mentor and a leader. This transformation is only possible if the mentor is clear about the responsibilities they have, as well as the role they play in portraying the part of a mentor-leader who is devoted to following a path of excellence.

Defining the Mentoring Relationship

The mentoring relationship experience is different for everyone. A mentor is best defined as a transformational leader, a person who nurtures the personal development within an individual or a group of people.

A mentor helps people overcome heavy obstacles in life that they otherwise could not remove themselves, as well as helping when necessary through advice, suggestions, and asking direct questions to elicit responses.

This path leads to a source of personal empowerment through working with other people. Over time the mentee builds a higher level of confidence through the consistent support and encouragement of a mentor.

This happens within the positive boundaries and depths of a relationship where two people are presented with a unique opportunity to do some real growing together. The relationship makes a huge difference in the quality of a person's life, and by working together toward similar goals, both partners benefit from sharing their experiences with each other.

"The delicate balance of mentoring someone is not creating them in your own image but giving them the opportunity to create themselves."

— Steven Spielberg

The goal of a mentoring partnership is building a relationship. It's not about business, money, or politics; it's about forming a lasting transformation through sharing ideas, thoughts, and feelings as the mentor passes on what they know to the next person that will carry on the message to future generations.

A mentor is someone who is passionate and enthusiastic about the role, and if the mentee picks up on this, they respond to the mentor's enthusiasm, opening up a high level of trust that allows the relationship to flow and expand further.

Mentoring is a unique blend of a deep, personal friendship, mutual growth, and an open and honest channel of communication with another human being through a discussion of issues surrounding both lives. Mentors are leaders who exhibit the changes they want to see in others.

A good mentor helps another person learn to tap in to their true potential for achieving higher levels of success. From business to family, and in relationships that evolve to form a solid partnership, a spiritual transition occurs.

Many people never try anything new or unique, not because they are incapable, but because they lack the support and encouragement to stand up and face their greatest enemy: themselves.

Mentoring is a solid investment with unlimited returns and maximum potential. By sharing knowledge and vision, we help others build visions of their own, creating their own successes, and in turn, they show others how to do the same.

The mentor who demonstrates patience, perseverance, and discipline realizes that not everybody evolves at the same pace emotionally or spiritually. As a mentor, understand that people take time to grow and that growth is often a painful, time-consuming process.

However, the results of these growing pains are astounding and contribute to the development of future generations to come. A mentee will shine when they are ready to show you who they are. When this day arrives, you will realize all the moments you invested in this person were well worth it.

Remember that you become what you give away to another. If you give only a small part of yourself, only that small part will grow and mature. You must share yourself completely and give as much as you can in order for people to grow and learn from your wealth of experience and sincerity.

Mentoring: Do You Have What It Takes?

> *"My mentor said, 'Let's go do it,' not 'You go do it.' How powerful when someone says, 'Let's!'"*
>
> **— Jim Rohn**

Mentoring is not a game of psychology or curing someone from any form of mental illness. We leave those jobs for the professionals.

The only qualification you must possess in order to do this effectively, and with the deepest impact, is to mentor people with sincere honesty and good intentions.

But Where Do I Begin? What Do I Need to Know?

Mentoring is about service and how willing and humble you are to do for others what you would not even do for yourself. To perform this service effectively, you must possess a balance of humility and strong personal values.

In addition, you must have excellent listening skills and experience that relates to the mentee, as well as a passion and love for supporting the growth of another individual without expectations or personal gain.

The focus is on the mentoring apprentice/partner, accepting this person as a whole, and helping them to get from where they are to where they want to be.

What Kind of Special Training Is Required?

You do not need special training to become a mentor; believing otherwise is a common misconception. All you need is a burning desire to help others. The only training, special skills, or knowledge required is what you already have with you: a lifetime of experience!

Yes, your experience is 80 percent of your training and you already have enough of it to begin mentoring today. It is your chance to help others begin the most exciting journey of their lives.

The best form of training is just doing it! Learn as you go. Show the mentee that you are not an expert or a know-it-all in the art of mentoring. You are just like them, and your goal is to help both of you succeed through a mutual partnership of friendship, trust, and commitment to a very special relationship.

Every mentor needs four basic qualifications:

- A passion for service in helping others to grow and succeed
- An investment of your time, as well as a solid commitment to the individual
- A desire to raise others up with the purpose of helping them to discover their true potential; the mentor's business is the development of people
- Good intentions: This is a genuine care/concern for others and a willingness to express empathy and patience

Focus on these, and you will be of great service to the people you are mentoring. See if you can add to this list by developing your own mentoring program for success.

The Mentor's Responsibility

One of the primary purposes for becoming a mentor is to help another become a mentor and a leader. This transformation is only possible if the mentor is clear about the responsibilities they have, as well as the role they play in portraying the part of a mentor-leader who is devoted to following a path of excellence.

The mentor wants what is best for the mentee and understands they have needs that must be fulfilled. There are certain obligations that should be considered in order to effectively manage and maintain a successful relationship.

The mentor shares in the burden of pain the protégé is experiencing, so both people grow and transform. The mentor's primary task is to listen, offer suggestions, and give insight into the problems or challenges the mentee is experiencing.

The effective mentor always operates from a level of responsibility that takes care of the mentee first. If their needs are being met within the relationship, they are learning firsthand how to mentor another person.

You are molding the mentee for success, and this is a heavy responsibility. It is this passing down of the mentoring torch that sets the foundation for the relationship, and in so doing, creates a legacy of winners committed to making the world a better place.

As mentors, leaders, and role models, we share a bond of commitment with our mentees that forms a strong path toward personal excellence. Your work is about the people, as is expressed in this message: once you have mastered the principles of success, your work is just beginning.

Once you have achieved the golden crown, it is time to pass it on to someone else. It isn't yours to keep. You must pass it on to others so your circle of influence continues to grow.

The path to becoming an effective mentor is through contributing to the effectiveness of others. If you want to grow, you must help another grow as well. If you want to succeed, show another what it means to succeed.

A Mentor for Everyone

Mentorship is a solid investment in character: your character and the character of another person. It is our greatest opportunity to not only pass on what we know, but to help another person succeed.

To take this a step further, think of a failure in your life. Was it personal finance? A relationship? Doing what you love? Whatever it is, write it down and remember how you failed. What were the factors that precipitated the failure? Was it a lack of knowledge? A lack of experience?

Do you think you could have succeeded if you'd had positive support from someone like a mentor?

Now that you have identified the reasons you failed, how can you help someone else succeed where you failed? This is what true mentorship is really about. You are not just teaching a mentee how to succeed in life, you are helping them navigate through rough waters that you've already experienced.

Your mistakes, while they may have cost you, can benefit another person. If you have children or plan to have children, imagine how much life experience you can share with them.

They will make their own mistakes on the journey, but your instructions as a mentor can make it a better trip. Whether we admit it or not, we all want a helping hand through difficult times.

Look for the opportunity to share your message and make a difference in someone else's life. One simple act of kindness, a hand that reaches down and helps another person up, will be remembered.

Building an Unforgettable Legacy

"If you look to your past or even your present to see why you are here or what your purpose is, you may get stuck in a limited view of yourself. Instead, look beyond your years here on earth, reconnect with the divine, and bring forth your soul's legacy into the present moment."

— Debbie Ford

Your legacy is the blazing trail that you leave behind for the world to follow. It is the end result of your life that others will look at. Everything you stood for is recognized in some special way by those who benefited from your contributions: family, society, and the environment, and in some cases, the impact is global.

The legacy you build is your gift to the world, a passing of the torch, so your knowledge, experience, talent, gifts, and compassion are not forgotten. Your work and the impact you delivered to the people you worked with is carried well into the future. Others will cherish and remember you for the actions you take today.

Don't Let Your Gifts Die

One of the greatest tragedies is that many people die without ever having really lived their life's true potential. They pass away with great songs that have never been played and poems that will never be whispered by anyone.

They hold on to what they have in hopes of preserving it somehow, but it simply dies with them. The next time you meet someone, even if it is only for the first time, give that person your complete attention. Create a positive impact right then and there.

Too many of us pass away quietly, like a flame snuffed out in the dark, having been afraid to burn as brightly as we could have.

Do not be afraid to light your candles and hold them high. If you have a song to play, play it as loud as you can; if you have a brush and paint, create a beautiful picture; if you have a knack for acting, be the most passionate performer on the stage; should you be a public speaker, let the people hear your voice for miles away.

When we leave this world, we take with us our experiences, talents, knowledge, wisdom, love, and passions. We take with us the kingdom of our soul and leave behind everything else.

Wouldn't you rather leave behind more than just assets, cash, and a few good memories? What if your legacy could survive for fifty years? A hundred years? A thousand years?

Imagine if you could change people's lives, give them a hope they never had before, and make a difference in the world through the work you did in the short time you were here on Earth.

You are capable of doing more than you think possible. You must live each day as if there is no other. Regardless of your present age, whether sixteen or sixty, it is never too late to become the change you visualize happening around you.

The only way your legacy is going to survive is for you to pass on what you know. You can only achieve this if you work hard to connect with the right people. The legendary people of this world who have passed remain in our memories for one reason: they made a significant difference in our lives.

They showed the world they cared and that they stood for something the world has grown to love and admire. They are the world's greatest examples of mentors and leaders who are still touching us in many ways, making a global difference for many years after they are gone.

Your legacy is not about what you possessed or how much power you had over other people. It is not about wealth or fame. It is, in its very essence, about sharing your gifts, talents, love, emotions, kindness, and passion with the world.

You don't have to be a world leader or a person of great wealth and power to leave behind something worthy and of great importance. You have everything you need already within you. All you have to do is dig it up and put it to good use.

Those who left behind unforgettable legacies also had equally powerful visions. Your legacy is your vision to the world, and it is the greatest gift you could ever give back. Your legacy is your story, and it contains the teachings of your life. Just as the acorn holds the life of the oak tree, so does your legacy encompass all that you are and ever will be.

Your life will be remembered for the impact you leave on people. It is the hope you instill in people, touching their hearts in such a way that they feel compelled to continue your life's instruction to the next generation.

"All good men and women must take responsibility to create legacies that will take the next generation to a level we could only imagine."

— Jim Rohn

People want to be inspired, and they want to know how to inspire others. Imagine that decades later, the people you helped were still passing it down to their protégés, friends, and family members. This is the incredible power of building a legacy through mentoring others.

There is really nothing like it. The greatest way to be remembered is to pass on everything you are and all that you have, so the people within your circle of influence can carry the torch in your name and all those who have gone before you.

The legacy you leave is like a blueprint for others to follow and pick up where you left off. It is your gift to the world and will continue to grow even when you are not around. And it is something you can take part in today. You don't have to be a world-class athlete, an inventor, or a multibillionaire to leave behind a legacy worth something.

You can have an impact on the people you share your life with. Those we meet from one day to the next are the ones we should be concerned about. Therefore, focus on who you are, remember what you stand for and believe in, and determine what you can do to make this world a place of great opportunity and transformation, and share that with those around you.

The Exponential Factor

If you mentor someone, you are investing valuable time and energy in another person's well-being. As you spend quality time with them by communicating, listening, and working through some of life's most complicated issues, you are making a deep contribution to every person who comes in contact with your circle of influence.

This is the true strength of mentoring. You can take even greater pride and satisfaction in mentoring others when you know you aren't just influencing their lives, but the lives of those who find their way into your circle of influence.

The impact of mentoring is an exponential formula for success. When you instruct people on how to be a mentor for someone else, that person takes what they know and passes it on. In time, your investment creates a wave of influence like the rippling effect of a stone thrown into a lake.

> *"My legacy is that I stayed on course...from the beginning to the end, because I believed in something inside of me."*
>
> **— Tina Turner**

The ripple starts out small and expands to larger and larger areas. If an investment is something you are looking for, you should start with your investment in other people and relationships that benefit the growth of all parties involved. There is really no telling where it will lead once you start reaching out and helping other people.

In order for your investment to work, you have to be willing to put in the time and work. Your investment in the growth of another person will someday pay back in dividends and grow to become larger than anything you could ever imagine.

A mentor's work has the potential to reach hundreds, thousands, and—eventually—millions of people. This is a process that takes place over years, decades, and multiple generations that could span hundreds of years.

Your work counts, and the passion you put into the growth and development of other mentors is a long-standing example of the values and commitment you represented. Long after you are gone, your investments will continue to grow, and there is no telling how far your circle of influence could extend.

This is the beginning of your legacy. There is, after all, nothing more rewarding than seeing the people in which you have invested your time and energy grow into healthy people who help others as they work toward success.

Designing Your Legacy

Make just a few minutes to consider your personal legacy. Imagine if this were your last day on Earth. By tomorrow you will be gone, and what remains is the memory of the person you were, the lives you helped to change, the inspiring message you stood for, and the contribution you made to this world.

Looking back on your life, you are seeing everything that you did for the first time, as if through a window to the past.

As you watch the old reruns of your life flash by, how do you feel about the legacy you are about to leave behind? What significance did you have? What could you do differently today that you never tried before?

It is hard to think of our lives as ending someday. We move through each day, expecting the next one to come about. It is life. We hope it lasts for as long as we can keep it going. So we do what we can in as little time as we can.

Now, how about your legacy? What is the impact you want to leave behind?

Whom do you want to influence? Who do you want to remember you, and what do you want them to remember you for?

With this vision, you can start taking actions that will make a profound change.

In as many words as you can, begin writing down the legacy you're going to create. Be sure to include your personal mission statement, your personal values, and the contribution you are making. Leave nothing out.

If you live your life in accordance with your dreams and commit to designing your destiny through ongoing development of character traits and values, you will have a legacy that speaks volumes about your life.

Don't just settle for a flicker in the darkness of a large and empty room. Light up the lives of people you meet and make yourself an unforgettable source of inspiration.

Developing Your Mentor Program

> *"If you want to be successful, find someone who has achieved the results you want and copy what they do and you'll achieve the same results."*
>
> **— Anthony Robbins**

Now that you know what it takes to become a mentor, your goal is to help people rediscover the best of themselves buried inside. To do this, you need a plan to reach the people you are trying to help. Whether or not you are a coach or a leader, knowing the people you want to reach is key to being able to help them.

Turning your curiosity into a driving passion to help people discover their absolute best potential is an amazing journey. Once you get hooked into helping people and you dedicate all your resources and energy into that, everything changes.

Everything.

My world shifted the day I stopped chasing money and started pursuing the happiness of other people. But to do that, I needed to shift my thinking. I revamped my purpose, and it shifted the actions I was taking.

Instead of focusing on my needs first, I put the needs of others first. I know, it wasn't easy, and it still isn't. But this trait of leadership is often overlooked. We may have good intentions, but those intentions can be shrouded in personal objectives.

Setting People Up for Success

Our future mentors—the men and women who will carry on our work—rely on us to lay down the foundational steps for success. So, here are eight steps for becoming a good mentor. You can use these steps if you are leading people in your business, your family, or people in your organization.

1. Show People the Unlimited Possibilities

As a mentoring leader, one of the ways to motivate and inspire future mentors is to share resources available that inspire success and achievement. To do this, encourage mentees to read the biographies of successful people who have overcome the odds, meet with other mentors, join a motivational seminar or a support group, or listen to motivational audio CDs. Share the most positive aspects of this life with your mentees.

If the mentee is struggling from a lack of self-esteem brought on by past experiences, this step is an opportunity to construct a positive foundation that builds faith and inspires hope.

2. Believe in Them!

Always believe the best in people and know that they are capable of inducing changes that will have a massive impact on the world someday. Believe in their potential for greatness instead of finding error and fault in things they do, and you can build up confidence, reinforcing the idea that anyone can do anything at any point in their lives.

When you believe in others, those you mentor will absorb the strength of your convictions. They will soak up your positive energy and be influenced by your actions and positive mental attitude.

Everyone is capable of so much more. A lack of belief is what stops them from doing, having, and becoming more. When they succeed, you succeed.

3. Identify Dreams and Underlying Passions

Everyone has a dream that has yet to be discovered. Work with mentees to help them find their deepest passions. Help them discover a way to set this passion on fire.

As the mentee's model for excellence, you can show them how to focus on this power in order to draw it out and bring it to life. In doing so, you will unveil their great purpose for living. This is the start of something exciting, which leads to the next step.

4. Create a Goal-Oriented Mindset

Teaching people the process of goal setting is one of the most exciting steps for both the mentor and the mentee.

Follow the steps to create a blueprint of goals for your partner. Show them how you have done this and the success you achieved from creating your own list of goals. Through establishing goals for the mentee, you will shape and mold the relationship on many levels.

5. Establish a Level of Commitment

A mentoring leader must be committed to the process of helping others succeed and exceed their potential for growth. There can be no half measures here. Show the mentee that you are 100 percent committed to the relationship, and they might surprise you by returning the same level of commitment.

This is the basis for securing and building a solid relationship. A commitment to excellence is one of the key pillars of success for individuals, corporations, and—of course—mentoring.

6. Encourage and Praise

Everyone needs to be reminded they are doing well and they are on the right track. Encouragement is the greatest therapy for keeping people motivated and interested in what they are doing.

A lack of encouragement reinforces low confidence, whereas words of praise build self-esteem and motivate people to walk with you the entire distance. People want to be appreciated and know their efforts are being observed by people who have taken an interest in their lives.

7. Be Accountable

As a mentor, our responsibility to our mentees continues even after they have moved on to create their own legacy. We still have an obligation, unless the relationship ends completely, to check in and see how they are doing. This might be via phone call, dropping by their house for a visit, or just sending a short email.

Instead of simply pushing people out into the world to take care of things their own way, the mentor should leave their door open for future contact and brief follow-ups on the success of their mentees. Relationships take hard work and effort, and we must maintain a certain level of accountability even after the mentee has moved on.

8. Be Strategic in Planning the Success of Your Mentorship.

How do you want to be remembered? What are some of the words you would like people to say about you at your funeral?

What actions will you take from now on that will move you in the direction of leaving behind a worthy legacy? What is the message you would like to pass on to future generations?

Take the time to think about this carefully and know exactly what it is you want to portray to the world, and then seek to become that person.

Identify the kind of person you want as a mentor. What personal qualities does this person have that you admire? What kind of a relationship are you hoping to develop with them?

What are the primary roles and responsibilities of a mentor? What would you expect from such a relationship? How would you contribute to making this a successful relationship with your mentor/mentoring apprentice?

Think about what your life means and the role you are fulfilling, and how you can use your experience and knowledge to help others.

What are some of the personal challenges you will encounter on your way to becoming a mentor?

What are your character weaknesses? What are your character strengths?

Write down three weaknesses holding you back and brainstorm ideas for overcoming them.

What kind of an influence would you like to have in the lives of other people?

What is the legacy you want to leave for others to follow?

What will your legacy stand for? What will it say about the kind of person you were?

Guidelines for Effective Leadership and Mentoring

The mentor leads by a set of principles that serve as guidelines for establishing the role of an effective mentor and leader. If you follow these principles, you will be successful in helping others achieve their goals and long-term successes.

As mentors, we must strive to attain certain vital characteristics if we are to become effective leaders.

The mentor is someone who:

- Helps to clarify and determine goals, and to build a vision that supports the success of those goals
- Shows the partner various methods to overcome life's obstacles, such as fear, procrastination, deeply rooted negative character habits, work-related stress issues, and relationship issues
- Helps to identify self-destructive habits and negative beliefs by offering suggestions or a course of action to take the mentee from a place of weakness to a place of personal empowerment
- Helps the partner in discovering and nurturing unique talents and interests so they can merge with their chosen path and fulfill their role in this world
- Listens with genuine interest to the partner and guides them to discover solutions to problems through asking pertinent questions related to their area of concern
- Encourages people to expand their horizons—that is, to stretch out into the world, pushing beyond their comfort zone so they are more comfortable with taking risks and trying new things
- Assists the mentee to build strong character values in line with the person they most desire to become

- Leads people to discovering a set of principles and ethics they can live by in order to become of greater value to society
- Shares their own unique experiences with the mentee, offering helpful insights while demonstrating a genuine enthusiasm and willingness to be there when needed
- Focuses on the individual, the complete person, and builds a relationship based on the principle that the health and well-being of the mentee comes first
- Teaches another how to become a good mentor
- Is committed to the relationship and the well-being of the mentee for as long as the relationship is active (this commitment forms a solid bond between both individuals)

How many of these traits are you strong in? Which traits need improvement? Take note of what you could work on to upgrade your mentoring leadership skills.

Section IV: The Master of Developing Creative Ideas

"Ideas can be life-changing. Sometimes all you need to open the door is just one more good idea."

— Jim Rohn

Ideas That Build the Future

> *"Your mind is for having ideas, not holding them."*
>
> **— David Allen**

In this book so far, you learned how to handle difficult obstacles holding you back. By becoming aware of the obstacles in your way, you can create a roadway to greater freedom. By struggling with less, you create more.

Then, the section on managing your time taught you how to put your energy to good use. By learning to value your time, you become less distracted and your thoughts act as better vessels to bring good opportunities your way.

We looked at mentoring and the impact this can have on future generations. By learning to discipline the core self, you approach people from a position of self-confidence that becomes a "want" for many. When others are drawn toward your confidence and genuine compassion, you can help them to discover the best of themselves.

Now, let's look at the power of creative ideas and how a disciplined system for capturing and implementing these idea goes a long way to helping you get anything you want. How is this possible?

Ideas are the spark of all creativity. By removing your obstacles, you free up your mind to think more creatively. By managing your minutes, you spend more time being creative and less time wasting your most precious resource: time. Then through mentorship, you can instruct other people to tap into their greatest ideas and come up with innovative ideas to reinvent and transform their lives.

Creating an Idea Organization System

By putting your best ideas into action, there is no telling what could happen on this journey. With this system in place, you will be able to forge greater ideas to create anything you want: mastering a skill, building a business, or implementing innovative products and services to help people lead better lives. Your ideas can build a gateway to a better future, your future, and the future of generations to come.

I love coming up with new ideas. As I write books and blog articles, so many of the ideas I dream up with every day are either about stories, outlines, or even book titles for new material.

If I were a painter, I'd come up with ideas for new pictures; if I were a fashion designer, I'd be working on ideas for a new clothing line; a game programmer would have tons of ideas for new games, or ideas for improving existing ones.

An online entrepreneur generates ideas to connect with people and build new products. A business leader comes up with ideas for launching a new product. A mother generates ideas to teach her children from home. Entrepreneurs develop ideas to expand their business and reach a larger audience with their message.

When you put your imagination to work, you have endless possibilities and opportunities for personal development. When you are passionate about the work you do or project that you're working on, ideas can flow with ease.

If you are stuck in a job you hate, your negative thoughts surrounding work make the creating process more difficult. You might be less motivated to put your ideas into action. So, find something you love to do and put your ideas into action to find a way to make a living from doing what you love.

Whatever your passion is, that is the platform you should focus your ideas on. But, as you will see, it is good to spread your ideas across other categories and platforms as well.

You don't have to restrict yourself to just one specific area of interest. My ideas tend to cover a broad spectrum: one day I'll have an idea for a book, and the next day it could be something for a new online business.

World-class Ideas That Matter

Why are ideas an integral piece to success? A strong idea carries the potential to develop into a world-class work of art, a book, a business, or the solution to a problem that helps thousands of people.

Have you ever had an idea that you just had to take action on? Do you have so many ideas every day that you feel overwhelmed and don't know what to focus on first? Or maybe you struggle to come up with unique ideas and you want to make it a habit to create more?

Remember this: your ideas matter. People are waiting for the next thing to help them add greater value to their lives. You don't have to come up with the next best light bulb or have thousands of ideas like Edison or Einstein.

But, with a clear mind focused on solving a particular problem, solution development, or building your "dream lifestyle," you do have the potential to come up with the answer for just about anything.

> *"Ideas are like rabbits. You get a couple and learn how to handle them, and pretty soon you have a dozen."*
>
> **— John Steinbeck**

You have a world of ideas and thoughts that you haven't discovered yet. More than just a "good thought," a great idea could be the right idea to open the doors of your dreams. Everything you have ever wanted could be on the other side of your greatest idea if you have the courage to pursue it.

Mark McCormack, the founder and chairman of IMG and a best-selling author, said, "If new ideas are the lifeblood of any thriving organization—and, trust me, they are—managers must learn to revere, not merely tolerate, the people who come up with those ideas."

Ideas are infinite. They create the future. Good ideas can create your future! Build a business, enjoy your work, or plan out your goals for the next ten years and generate ideas for putting an action plan into the works.

The world was created based on the ideas of people with the courage to take action on them. In fact, with the information age here and new technology being developed every day, creative ideas are needed more than ever. And you never really know what you can turn out when you start to piece things together with your imagination and, when your creative subconscious bottled up inside you decides to make its presence fully known.

Building Your Own Reality

When you stop believing in the world's version of reality, and you set out to create your own reality that fills you up with a deeper sense of passion and purpose, a new life starts to take shape. Just look at all the entrepreneurs out there who have fashioned whole new careers and businesses because they had an idea and put it into action. You can create a similar experience if you know what it is that you want to create, and you put your ideas into action.

Taking confident action is imperative. You can have the greatest idea in the world, but if it just sits there at the back of your mind waiting for "someday," nothing will come of it. Action makes results happen. If you are not happy with the path you are on, it is up to you to change directions or take a new road altogether. It is never too late, and you are never too young or too old.

A lot of people lack confidence in their ideas. We hear names like Einstein, Edison, Jobs, and Disney and immediately think genius. Yes, these innovators were geniuses in their contributions to the world. This doesn't mean that you and I should shy away from creating an idea platform full of mind-blowing inventions that others might pay money for. Is it really too hard to believe?

Mai Lieu was a hair stylist in a salon twelve years ago when she had an idea for a self-styling gadget that would save people a ton of money. She quit her job and worked on her invention, the CreaClip. Now she is a successful millionaire entrepreneur, speaker, and author.

Susan Gregg Koger turned her passion for thrifting and vintage clothing into a thriving business by selling the finds she could no longer keep around her home. The company called ModCloth is growing at the rate of 40 percent a year with over 450 employees.

Imagine what you could do if you put your ideas to work. What ideas have you had that you dismissed as silly or unimportant because you didn't think it mattered?

A good idea is not always surrounded by an "aha" moment or feelings of euphoria. Many times, they are like nuggets buried in the earth that go unnoticed for thousands of years until someone sees the value in these nuggets, pulls them out of the dirt, and puts them into action.

You have a "nugget" within you right now, an idea that could change the direction of everything. You just haven't discovered it yet. Or maybe you have, and you're afraid to talk about it. Some ideas pull at us for years, which could be referred to as a calling to do something that cannot be ignored.

You have the powerful urge to do something different with your life that serves a greater purpose. Your ideas are like stones leading to that higher calling.

You can make a difference right now by sitting down for one hour and sketching out all the ideas you've had over the past week. Try it and see. Do it right now. Grab a pen and paper and brainstorm the ideas that have been roaming around in your mind. I'll bet you've had several good ones since this morning. Don't cast aside your ideas just because they seem "out there" or too unbelievable.

By exercising your idea muscle, you will make idea generation a habit. Soon you will have so many ideas that you won't have time for idle chitchat or small talk that leads nowhere. You'll be too busy building a better future for yourself.

One reason many people fail to succeed is because they fail to trust in their own imagination. Relying on cheap entertainment and distractors to fill in the time, they become lost in the hustle of looking busy but they're not. You must begin to believe and then to trust. Can you remember a time when your creative flow was in high gear? How long ago was that?

Return to that moment again in time and relive the dream you had at one time in your life. What ideas were you working on? What did you want to do and be? By going deep and doing a self-exploration of your inner world, you will see the ideas, the nuggets, hiding there waiting to be called for.

The Idle Mind and Banishing Excuses

An idle mind without a purpose will develop all sorts of bad habits: excessive TV watching, compulsive shopping, addictions such as gambling or worse. Without this focus in your life, you will look for distractions to fill up the time or create trouble for the sake of doing something.

Don't get sucked into the boredom life trap. Focus on turning good ideas into a creative funnel that adds value to people's lives and you'll be taking the first real step toward bringing your uniqueness into the world.

When people say they are bored, what they really mean is they want to do something but don't know what to do. If they can't occupy the mind with a creative project or put an idea into action, it opens the door to a host of negativity.

"Focus on the journey, not the destination. Joy is found not in finishing an activity but in doing it."

— Greg Anderson

Getting focused and keeping your goals in sight will keep your ideas flowing continuously. They will be overflowing and you won't be able to keep up. You have lots of good ideas and some great ones. Now, you are going to explore various ways to capture, organize, and integrate these ideas.

But first, you need to get your excuses out of the way. Instead of creating the excuses below, you could be creating your future.

My ideas are not original, creative, or mind-blowing. (That's okay; you can build from existing platforms. You don't have to come up with something totally unique. Just find a better way to do it.)

All the good ones are already taken. (No, they aren't. The world needs ideas now more than ever. This is the worst excuse I hear the most often.)

- I'm not an inventor. (Learn how to invent and patent; Mai Lieu did.)

- It takes me a long time to come up with a good idea for anything.

- Most of my ideas are crap. (Yes, maybe they are, but most ideas are until you find a good one.)

- I'm not good at writing ideas down; I get them and then I forget about them. (Don't worry; we will cover the idea capturing system soon.)

- I need an MBA in order to launch a successful business. (Steve Jobs never finished college, and Einstein never finished high school. So?)

- Whenever I have a good idea, it turns out somebody has already taken it. What's the point? (True, a lot of ideas out there are similar, and it's not uncommon for people to have the same idea. But that's okay. The fact that you came up with a really good idea that someone else did says something: you can do this!)

- People laugh when I tell them about an idea I had. I don't have much confidence in myself to really come up with anything that's worthy. (You might be telling the wrong people. Join a mastermind group that supports your ideas. People don't laugh at you but laugh with you.)

- There are lots of excuses people use to talk themselves out of doing something. We seem to think that all the good ideas are taken, or that only inventors, scientists, and creatives have the right to come up with all the good stuff that changes the world.

You don't have to come up with an idea that is going to change the world. If you do, that's great, but take the pressure off yourself to come up with something that is so unique nobody else has ever thought of it.

Most ideas these days are built from existing platforms that other inventors and creatives have already established. This means you can look at something that is working for other people and try to find an edge; look for a way that it can be done better. That is where your ideas exist!

One of the best ways that you can do this is to create a business, product, or service that solves problems for people. When was the last time someone helped you with a problem? I'll bet it was a book, blog, or product that you purchased? Or maybe a friend of yours gave you some advice that you followed through on.

Keep a positive mindset and you'll stay focused on putting your thoughts and ideas into action. From there, you can funnel your plan into a business of your choice.

Capturing Ideas on the Move

"The test of a first-rate intelligence is the ability to hold two opposed ideas in mind at the same time and still retain the ability to function."

— F. Scott Fitzgerald

One of the most important daily habits you can have for your ideas is to develop a system for gathering and compiling everything into one central location. Once you get into the habit of generating ideas for your business, lifestyle, hobby, or life's passion, you'll find your "idea machination" exploding.

It is natural and exciting. Imagine walking down the street and suddenly getting an idea for something that completely excites you. Then, ten minutes later, you totally forget what it was and you can't recall it no matter how hard you try. The trick is, you have to write it down or record it right away.

If you don't take action right away and get your idea down on paper or recorded into digital software, when you try to recall it later, you won't be able to. This has happened to me many times. I lost a lot of good stuff this way that I couldn't recall hours later when I wanted to.

Fortunately, with today's simplicity of taking notes on handheld devices, you can have an entire system for note collecting and idea gathering without skipping a beat.

After all, what's the point of having good ideas if you can't remember them?

This is why it is essential to have an **idea journal**. By creating a system where you capture your ideas on the run, you can avoid losing those golden moments when a good idea that could be worth cash in your hand suddenly materializes in your mind.

What Is an Idea Capturing System?

It could be an idea journal with pen or paper or digital software, such as an idea app, where you record your ideas. (I am old school and still love writing down my ideas in an idea journal).

By opening up the app on your computer or smartphone, you can plug in your idea for easy access later. You can also use the recording mic to speak your ideas into your phone (more on this later).

Then, when you are working on a particular project or this week's goal, you can access your ideas easily and quickly, pull them up, and put them into action through idea expansion and building a set of action steps around the idea.

There are countless ways you can record your ideas without risk of losing them. If you think you can get away with trying to remember your idea that you just had, your memory is a lot better than mine. I have so many ideas throughout the day for books, blogs, and strategies to grow my business that I couldn't possibly manage on memory alone.

Even geniuses such as Edison and Einstein had to record their ideas because they had thousands of ideas that would otherwise be lost. In fact, Thomas Edison had so many ideas that an organization was founded called the Thomas A. Edison Papers Project committed to organizing and editing his life's works. In fact, these notebooks and documents are still being investigated today.

Idea Capturing Systems

When you try to recall that same idea later on in the day, you'll find, in most cases, you can't. Believe me, I have lost many good ideas this way. They were great thoughts "in the moment," but when I didn't record them, I had forgotten what they were an hour later. Make capturing your ideas a habit, and don't rely on memory alone.

Here is the process you are going to use for capturing and putting your ideas into action:

1. Capture/record ideas
2. Organize ideas into folders
3. Initiate and take action

Now, I still love the pen and paper method. There is just something about writing it down that makes it more real and just adds more juice to your thinking process and memory retention. You actually retain things more when you put pen to paper. The physical process of writing stuff down actually makes it more real. When you allow your imagination to free flow, your subconscious takes over.

But because I don't always have my journal notebook with me, I use the apps discussed here throughout the day. Then, at the end of the day, I'll write out the ideas I had during that day. I keep an idea journal that I record all the good stuff in. I use this as a reminder for ideas that I want to take intentional action on. You can also use this for free flow writing.

Free Flow Writing Method

Take thirty minutes and start to write. If you can't think of what to write about, just start with anything. Don't stop to think or edit what you write. Just let the writing flow uninterrupted. You can write about a topic you are interested in, or an idea that you want to try out and develop.

I recently read a book about waking up early in the morning and getting things done. So, based on this, I wrote a free flow article about all the benefits of waking up early. Then, I started to come up with ideas for what I can do if I wake up early. This led into an action plan I could initiate. My idea then expanded into the ways I could set my mornings up to wake up early and take immediate action with a set routine.

Make free flow writing a daily habit. You can do this first thing in the morning when you get up or throughout the day using small pockets of time. This exercise really digs deep and gets the good stuff out of your mind. It's like "mining" for the ideas that are in there. Before you know it, things that you had never thought of are hitting the paper.

You can use the **Pomodoro technique** and set a timer for twenty-five minutes during this structured time start your free flow writing. At the end of the twenty-five minutes, you can either stop or take a five-minute break and then continue for another twenty-five minutes.

I do these sessions three times a week where I will schedule my "idea creating" time so anything that is in my head I can get out and then work with it much easier. Here is the Pomodoro technique website so you can learn more about all the benefits of this great little system.

Free Flow Writing Action Tasks:

Schedule 20-30 minutes a day to do free flow writing. If you have nothing to write about, quickly scan some blogs or articles. Or dig into your ideas folder or idea journal and pull out an idea.

This is a great way to start taking action on your idea. Be sure to schedule your time for this, or else it will be something that you'll do "when you have time," and then it won't get done.

So, collect during the day, and organize your ideas throughout the day or at night. Initiate your thoughts when the time is right. Set aside ten minutes for idea implementation. With this strategy, you can master your ideas and grow the habit of putting them into an organized system.

I don't want to overload you with choices, so I'll give you four more software options and you can choose from your favorite.

To learn more about the free flow method and morning pages, you can check out one of favorite books on ideas and generating creativity—***The Artist's Way*** by Julia Cameron.

Captio App

This app is great when you are on the run and need to deliver quickly. The app is simple to implement. When you get an idea, simply open it up on your phone, type in the note, and hit send. Done. It goes right to your email inbox. You can take pictures as well. This app integrates with other apps as well such as Evernote. You can work on or offline and it will store your notes until you're ready to send.

Simple Mind

This is an Android app to record your most creative ideas. People who are visual learners will find this a useful tool for organizing thoughts and ideas and customizing everything in an easy-to-visualize mind map. You can customize your experience with a wide range of connection and node designs.

Simple Mind is a practical and simple interface where you can directly draw nodes and the connections between them using touch gestures. You can save your creations and access them later, although you won't be able to export them to any external formats. But this doesn't, prevent you from taking screenshots of the diagrams you make.

Brainsparker

This is an app I've been using for several years and it's fantastic: Brainsparker is an iOS app that helps you think outside the box with a series of images, quotes, and questions. Because it encourages new thinking, cultivates fresh ideas, and pushes users to think outside the box, Brainsparker is an excellent resource for creators that need a daily dose of motivation and inspiration. You can use this solo or with groups to brainstorm and generate loads of fresh ideas ready to be implemented.

Create a Swipe File

According to Wikipedia, a Swipe file is:

A collection of tested and proven advertising and sales letters. Keeping a swipe file (templates) is a common practice used by advertising copywriters and creative directors as a ready reference of ideas for projects. Copywriters are not the only ones who can benefit from having a swipe file.

As book publishing coach Diane Eble points out, authors and publishers can benefit from creating a swipe file of best-selling titles to give them ideas for their own titles. Publicists can create a swipe file of great press release headlines. Swipe files are a great jumping-off point for anybody who needs to come up with lots of ideas.

Creating a swipe file is another good idea for collecting ideas, resources, and information to be used on upcoming projects.

How to use a swipe file

Swipe files are great for gathering information related to ideas you have or projects you are working on.

Writers use swipe files to collect ideas on existing book titles. Business managers use swipe files to collect data and information on how to improve profit margins. Designers use swipe files to gather ideas for pictures and ideas related to new artistic projects. If you are in a profession that demands you store information, ideas, or resources, a swipe file is necessary to keep everything together.

You can create a swipe file for just about anything you are working on: projects at work, a website, or organizing a workshop. Swipe files are great for keeping track of your ideas that you can implement later on down the road. A swipe file can be anything used from magazines, websites, or catalogues, and can be composed of pictures, articles, or your original ideas.

Keep in mind that a swipe file is a collection of ideas from other sources and can be used for inspiration or information storage. In addition, it is a clear record of resources that you might use and can be referred to later on for citing or bibliographic purposes.

Each swipe file is unique and can be used to collect articles, snippets, or pictures for reference depending on the type of work you do. Swipe files are great for inspiration and can be used to brainstorm or provide inspiration for creativity.

The Whitman Strategy

This is a strategy that the American poet, essayist, and journalist Walt Whitman used to organize his ideas. Similar to our digital formats of organizing into folders, this is another great alternative to keeping your ideas in physical location.

While it's great to keep everything backed up and organized using apps and digital devices, many people are still prefer keeping notebook journals or, in the case of the Whitman strategy, categorizing ideas and keeping them separated according to whatever projects you are working on.

Whitman, whenever he had an idea, would write it down on paper and place in an envelope according to the category. Later on, when he needed an idea, he would pull out the slips of paper from the envelopes and piece them together. This might seem old school compared to today's methods of recording

(Evernote, note-taking apps, or using Word), but the system is solid and adds to the fun of idea gathering and organizing.

Some people like to keep their ideas in physical form, and if you do, the Whitman strategy works great. Another variation to this is to use a large binder with plastic sleeves. Each sleeve or pocket would be used for a different category.

You can adopt another similar strategy by using files as well and keeping them in a cabinet. The Whitman strategy of using envelopes doesn't require much space, and you can set it up quickly.

Building Your
Idea Organization System

"Enthusiasm is the yeast that makes your hopes shine to the stars. Enthusiasm is the sparkle in your eyes, the swing in your gait. The grip of your hand, the irresistible surge of will and energy to execute your ideas."

— Henry Ford

Now I'm going to show you a productive system for organizing your ideas so you can find them when you need to. Without a system for locating the right ideas at the right time, you'll waste time scrolling through the numerous files and folders, wondering where you put them.

Spare yourself the frustration and create a simple system to access your ideas when you need them. With a simple system in place, you'll be able to keep everything organized for easy access later.

In David Allen's book *Getting Things Done: The Art of Stress-free Productivity*, he says that when you organize your papers in the office, you should only touch a paper twice: once when you receive it and the second time when you put it into its appropriate folder. If not, you end up shifting papers around to find it. This is counterproductive. Things get lost. Time is lost.

This same system applies to your ideas as well. **The worst place to keep ideas is in your mind.** You need a better place to store your ideas so they can be accessed right away without trying to remember the great idea you had the other night when you were out with your friends.

Just as every piece of paper needs to be filed away so it doesn't get lost, your ideas need be stored digitally as well. You need an organized storage and retrieval system for those ideas.

Without a system, your ideas will end up everywhere, and when you try to recall that "thought you had last week," finding it is going to be difficult. In the last chapter, you learned how to capture your ideas; now you have to know where and how to store them so they can stay parked until you're ready for taking action (more on this later).

When you are busy dumping your notes into a folder, if you don't take the time to organize them at the end of the day or week, you'll end up with a big mess and finding what you want will be time consuming. If you don't do something with them, notes will be everywhere and possibly spread across various apps or buried in other folders on your desktop, which adds to the confusion.

To avoid this, the next stage is to have a system for organizing these ideas so they stay current and easily retrievable

Remember there are three steps, I already covered the first one—having a system in place to capture your ideas—so now I am going to cover the next one—a place to put the ideas.

The first step you have already covered by having a system in place to capture your ideas. Now, you need a place to put the ideas so they're in the right folders. You already know how a filing cabinet works:

1. Loose paper is found in office.
2. Paper goes into folder in filing cabinet.
3. Folder is located with a stack of other folders (This might be a project you are working on or related subjects.)
4. When information or a document is needed regarding this particular client or contract, the file is opened up and the contents taken out.

Simple, right?

Okay then, let's take a look at how you can store your ideas in digital and physical format.

I collect ideas by dividing them into categories. It works like this: Organize a group of folders and label each one according to the specific category, niche, or project. You can loop your ideas together if they are to be used in the same project or work. This is a process also known as cross-fertilization that Edison employed when he was working on several projects or inventions at the same time.

For example, I have a folder for blog ideas, books, and website development. There are so many ideas here as well as resources I have to access that I have multiple folders for each category.

Whatever your ideas focus on, or the project you are working on is, this is how you should structure your folders.

The key is to have a place where you can store your ideas that are related to similar projects, interests, and passions. I know this seems logical and very elementary but nothing can be worse than looking for something and not being able to find it. Even if you are not an organized person, this system can help you to get organized. It is not overly complex and can be managed easily if you follow the process.

Once your idea is recorded, whether it is written down in a notebook or in an app while on the run, you then move it one more time to the folder/category where it belongs.

The Three-Step Folder Strategy

The three-step folder strategy is a simple system for gathering your ideas, organizing them into the right folders, and then moving your folders into an active funnel.

This is how it works:

Create one folder. This is called the "Three-Step Folder-Main" (or you can call it whatever you want). But this folder's function is to place your three folders for your ideas.

Make three folders inside the main folder. You can do this as a stack in Evernote or create three folders in Google Drive or on your desktop. However, just note that storing information on your desktop only is risky without backup. Make sure it is stored in the cloud at least.

Now, here is a breakdown of the folders (or notebooks) and how to use them.

Three-step folders recap:

1. Capture your ideas in one central notebook. Set this up on your desktop with backup in the Cloud, Google Drive or Evernote.

2. Go back at the end of the (day) week and purge this folder, shifting ideas into their proper folder categories by moving them into the second folder. Create a mind map and start to put your project into focus.

3. When you decide to take massive action, you move a project's subfolder from your second folder into the third folder. Create. From here you can sketch out your action plan. Include all the other material you collected: articles, swipe files, and links.

4. ABC: Always Be Creating!

Setting Up Projects and Idea Implementation

"First comes thought; then organization of that thought, into ideas and plans; then transformation of those plans into reality. The beginning, as you will observe, is in your imagination."

— Napoleon Hill

Working on a project that you are passionate about is when the ideas really begin to take shape. By now, you should have your idea folders for various niches and/or categories. Don't worry if you only have a few folders set up. This is a creative process that never ends.

The important thing is that you have started setting up your ideas so they can be put into action when needed. If you haven't over the course of the next few weeks, try to get your system set up so you can have an organized, logical flow to capturing and implementing all your thoughts.

It is great when you can start a project of any kind (web course, building a new house, or landscaping your garden outside) and you already have a solid idea where to begin because of the ideas you have been keeping in your ideas folder or swipe files.

When you do start a project that you have been collecting research data, ideas, and interviews for, just go into your central folder (you have one, right?) and pull everything out that is related to that project (remember the Whitman strategy).

I make a central folder for the project I am working on and place it in the center of my desktop. Then, every time I sit down at the computer to do some work, everything I need is right there.

Just a note on desktops: clear everything off except the project you are working on or core ideas related to your current work. Desktop clutter halts your efficiency and distracts you.

Now, when it comes to your ideas for a particular project, you will have lots of ideas for other stuff too (cross fertilizing). This is great because you can start building other projects and contributing to their development at any time even if you won't be starting that project for months or even years later.

The only disadvantage to this is that you will be tempted to start something new every time you have a new idea. I fall into this trap where if I am struggling with a certain project and I can't find the solution to a problem or I get stuck, I'll start something new.

Why? New ideas are exciting! This is especially true if the project you are working on becomes challenging (and it will) or you just want a break from it. There is nothing wrong with taking a break from your current work, but don't let the break turn into a few months.

Over the years, I had lots of half-finished projects and start-ups sitting around because I would start something, get halfway and take a break, then go do something else. Some projects I went back and finished and some are still waiting to be completed.

Unless you are a project manager and you have to run several projects at once, I'd recommend you take all your ideas from one project and put them into action for that one project only. This cuts down on the chatter and noise of having to deal with so many action steps happening at the same time.

As you come up with ideas for other related projects, throw them into your ideas folders or make a swipe file for them and then leave it. You can go back to them later on when you are ready to put them into action.

Get into the "singular focus" mode and stay there. Work on your idea until you have a complete mind map of ideas and related topics surrounding your project. And I mean any project, big or small. Your project might only take you a few days to complete, or it might take several months.

Stretching yourself too thin by working on several projects at the same time and then failing to finish any of them will cause frustration and a lack of motivation. By sticking with one project or task at a time, and working through to completion, you are going to feel motivated to start the next one right away. This boosts your confidence, and by using up your ideas for that one project, you can shift focus to the new project once the present one is finished.

I use the "singular focus" method and try to stay tuned to one area of work until it is finished. This is a very powerful habit to develop. You might have a project that has several "parts" or "sub-projects," depending on its scope and size, and that is okay, but stick within the framework of your current project. If you start something new before finishing what you are working on, you'll lose momentum for the project you started.

If you do get stuck on something, take some time to do more research or further your knowledge. You might want to expand on your mind map and get some new ideas happening that can build your momentum again. Once completed, you will experience a boost of energy that propels you to get to that finish line and wrap things up.

Just think about the massive surge in confidence and energy you'll have if you:

- Complete your book
- Create an online course
- Open up your own business

- Launch your website
- Make an addition to your new home
- Finish your master's degree
- Design a new product

Now, some projects do require years to complete. While the scope of this book doesn't cover projects in real depth, you can manage several projects at once if one of them is long term like working on a master's degree (two–four years) and the other is short term such as creating an eBook or training manual (three–six months).

Action Plan

Use singleness of purpose and planning to focus on one project at a time. Pull out your ideas for this project and start to form the foundation for your work by piecing together the ideas.

Add to your information and then more ideas will continue to flow in. Stay focused on the one project and finish it, using up all your ideas and depleting your ideas folder for this work. You will be more confident, have more energy, and feel great about your work as you continue to push ahead.

Creating a Mind Map: Your Idea Expansion Tool

A mind map is a great way to turn your ideas into a viable course of action. With a mind map you are performing a brain dump of all the ideas you have for your project. I would highly recommend putting all of your core ideas to the mind map test. How it works is simple and fun.

You place your main idea in the center of the page. I would recommend that you do this on a large piece of paper or board that is either spread out on the floor or tacked to the wall. This way you can work at it standing up and you can move around more freely.

The purpose of this is to get all your ideas down on paper in one big brain dump. Once done, you can step back and see what you have. You'll be amazed the stuff that can come out of your head when you focus on one core concept for a fixed amount of time.

Previously, I mentioned using the Pomodoro Timer technique. I like this system because it sets a fixed time where you focus on just the one task. Again, set up your timer for twenty-five minutes and get cracking. See how many ideas you can dump out onto your mind map schematic in this short amount of time.

Here is what you do to set up your mind map:

Materials

Tack up some poster paper on the wall. Prepare Post-it Notes and a marker. Use a timer to blast your ideas out for a set amount of time.

Write Down Your Main Idea in the Center

At the center of the board, I write down the main idea that I want to generate ideas for. If it is a book, you would write down the tentative title; if it is an idea for a course you want to create, write down the idea you have for the course, such as "How to build a website." If it is a family vacation, you can write down the name of the place you are visiting. Decide on your main idea and get ready.

Set a timer for twenty minutes. For that time only, branch out from the central idea and connect all the other ideas associated with the main idea. Within several minutes that blank paper looks like a wild maze or a spider web. I usually put each idea in its own bubble, too. Each bubble represents an idea and that might also have sub-ideas that could branch off from it.

Work for twenty–twenty-five minutes to get everything down on paper. I find that I start to slow down at the twenty-minute mark. Once you get some practice in, you can go at it for thirty minutes. This can be an exhausting activity but definitely worth it. This is how I prepare for all my books or blogs; I also use it for planning weekend trips or doing work around the house.

Don't stop to worry about the order or whether what you have written down is any good. You don't have to edit a mind map. Just create and keep pulling thoughts and ideas out of your head. You can use the ideas in your map to identify the actions you can start taking right away.

If this is a project that you're working on, what actions can you see based on the mind map that you could take today? Stand back and look at the work you have done.

Once you have your mind map ready, you might want to transfer it to your digital platform. It's not necessary, but if you'd like to make it look a bit cleaner, creating the same mind map in an app would be a good option.

Action Steps

- *Focus on one project at a time; finish it up and move onto the next one.*
- *Keep moving all your ideas into their folders that are related to all future projects and work.*
- *Use the mind map strategy to brain dump all your ideas about a goal or project onto your board. Keep working until you have filled up the page or board with all your ideas.*
- *Step back and analyze what you have created. Then try to visualize the action steps you can begin taking and put them in logical order.*

Building on Existing Platforms

"The ideas I stand for are not mine. I borrowed them from Socrates. I swiped them from Chesterfield. I stole them from Jesus. And I put them in a book. If you don't like their rules, whose would you use?"

— Dale Carnegie

Many of the inventions and innovations you see and use every day originated from someone's idea. But chances are they weren't just one person's ingenuity but were built over years of idea building, innovation, and cross-fertilization. This is what happens when an idea evolves over time.

It is a long-accepted belief that only creative people have great ideas, and that in order to be successful, you have to come up with something totally original that nobody else has ever thought of.

While innovative and creative ideas that completely change the world may be the rarity, most inventions or successful ventures are built on the ideas and concepts of others. In other words, you can build your business or brand from scratch, or you can create something from one of the thousands of existing platforms already out there.

Apple co-founder Steve Jobs created the iPod out of a need that he saw in the marketplace. But he wasn't the first to come up with the concept of "digital music." Who did?

The first official audio player was made by a company called Audio Highway and released in 1997. Other companies introduced several other audio devices, but they never got it right.

Steve Jobs took what had failed and what others had failed to take advantage of and turned it into a great product that has since become the biggest selling music device in the world with over 300 million sold.

Henry Ford was an American industrialist and founder of the Ford Motor Company. But Ford didn't create the automobile or the assembly line that would later become standard technology utilized around the world; he did, however, take advantage of the technology that already existed and created an automobile (the Model T) that sold for $825.00 and could be purchased by the average wage earner.

Ford took what had already existed and revolutionized the automobile industry by giving everyone what they wanted: a car that the average middle-class family could afford. His assembly line became synonymous with the mass production of inexpensive goods that changed the way companies operated globally.

Ray Kroc, who gave Big Macs to the world, purchased the rights to McDonald's from the McDonald brothers who had already built it into a successful restaurant in San Bernardino, California.

After selling eight mixers to the McDonald brothers at their store location, he looked at the potential of the operation and knew there was definite massive potential if the business were handled properly. The McDonald brothers were reluctant to go big with the franchise, so Kroc bought the brothers out and put his idea into full forward motion.

Kroc implemented his plan and worked hard to bring his vision to reality: a chain of restaurants lined up and down the streets serving food to America. The McDonalds had the right idea; they just didn't want to expand on it.

Ray Kroc did.

It has since grown to over 35,000 restaurants worldwide in 118 countries. Remember, Ray Kroc started out with an idea that turned into a vision; the vision spawned a dream, and when he started to take action, his dream was fully realized.

Harland Sanders had a great fried chicken recipe and had the idea of selling it to restaurants. He drove across America for two years, pitching his recipe to restaurant owners. After getting over a thousand rejections, one restaurant owner finally said yes.

Now, KFC is the world's second largest restaurant chain after McDonald's, with 18,875 outlets in 118 countries and territories all using Colonel Sanders's secret recipe he thought up. Whatever you think up, resolve that you will persist until your ideas manifest into action. Work each day toward your goals, and never give up.

Just imagine what you can do if you pursue your ideas? What would happen if you put your vision into action? What would happen if you take intentional action every single day toward your dreams? What would your idea be worth if you put it out there and did something with it?

I want you to really think about this. Visualize the idea you have for something, whether it is a small business or applying a skill you have to sell to customers through such sites as Upwork, Freelancer, or Fiverr.

With some hard work and personal innovation, you can create a totally new way of life for yourself. Perhaps leave your crummy nine to five and start working for yourself? Think about it while you work through your ideas.

Imagine as if each idea you have is a “brick” in the creative funnel of your life. It is a piece of real estate with true value that, if applied the right way, could lead to the one thing in your life that you have always wanted.

Take a look around at some of the systems you see and look for the potential to make them better. This can be a system in your company or school, it can be a product or invention, or you can meet an unfulfilled need by implementing your own ideas and creating the best solution possible.

Always look for ways to improve on something, then look to see how you can make it your own.

Fourteen Areas to Generate Ideas

"Humility, I have learned, must never be confused with meekness. Humility is being open to the ideas of others."

— Simon Sinek

Now, let's take a look at the different ways you can get your "idea train" moving. By collecting your ideas and coming up with new ideas every day, your head will soon be spinning, and you will feel that push to do something.

Let's get some ideas going. It doesn't have to be a subject that you already know something about. Try coming up with ideas for topics that you know almost nothing about to get the mind muscles working.

I really want you to just unleash yourself here. Don't stop to think about how realistic it is or if your idea sounds foolish. Self-criticism is the one obstacle that prevents most people from accomplishing or following through with anything. They start to doubt themselves before they have given it a chance.

Here are some subjects you can start with to brainstorm your ideas. Try to come up with at least ten ideas for each one. See if any of these resonate with you. Check out the links to the websites as well.

1. Earning More Money

Write down ten ideas you have for making more money. This can be anything from having a yard sale to becoming an affiliate advertiser. Now, take one of these ideas and brainstorm how you are going to earn more money. Will you set up a shop on eBay? Do you have any ideas for investing your money? There are thousands of ways you can increase your income. You don't have to settle for your "fixed" salary.

2. Building Self-Confidence

Write down ten ideas you have for improving your self-confidence. Try one of these ideas right now. Write this idea down on paper and keep it with you all day tomorrow. In what areas of your life do you lose confidence? Is it in your relationships? Is it a situation at work? Is it something about yourself? Identify the area of your life that needs a confidence boost, and then write down your ideas for targeting this one specific point.

3. Losing Weight

Write down five ideas you have for losing weight. Imagine if somebody asked you for advice on how they could lose weight. How could you lose five pounds in a month? What exercises would you recommend?

Try to come up with at least twenty ideas and rank them in order of effectiveness. This is one of the big problems that millions of people struggle with. What if you could come up with a process or program to make losing weight fun and easy?

4. Writing a Book

Write down ten ideas you have for books you want to write. These can be books in your field of expertise or fiction titles that you've always longed to see written and published. Then, come up with ten ideas for marketing your book.

Nowadays with today's self-publishing revolution, creating your dream of writing a book is a real possibility. Thousands of people are launching their books daily. Will you be one of them?

You can follow this simple process for getting your book written fast:

- Mind map your ideas

- Create an outline
- Write for one hour a day for thirty days.

5. Ideas for Solving Current Problems

What problems do you often come across? Imagine if you could get paid for solving other people's problems? This is where websites, eBooks, and courses excel. Once you have figured out the strategies for delivering solutions to people's problems, you can start to make money. They will pay you for a solution! Write down several problems that people have, and then brainstorm several ideas that could solve this problem.

6. Time Management and Productivity

Do you waste time every day on menial tasks and distractions? Is this costing you time and money? Write a list of five–seven ideas to implement that focuses on timesaving and how you can manage your time better. If you believe that time really is money, then saving time is worth every penny.

I'll give you an example. I took a typing course so I could type faster. By doubling my typing speed, I can get more material out faster and make more money with my writing. What ways can you save time? Less TV? Make a list of time savers you can do or time wasters you can stop doing.

7. Health and Exercise

What ideas can you come up with to start getting in great shape? What ideas do you have to improve muscle tone, cardio, or your flexibility? Write down your ideas on how to get into shape and drop them into your "exercise" folder. Do you want to lose weight, or start on a paleo diet?

When it comes to your health and exercise, there are no limits to the ideas you can come up with. There is also a massive market for books, videos, and training manuals. This is something to consider if there is something you can offer people and try to start up a business by becoming an authority in a specific area.

8. Education and Learning

What ideas do you have about changing the way education is taught in our schools? The way people are learning is taking a major shift. Now, write down seven–ten ideas you would implement if you were given the mission to change the way education is being taught.

What would you do? How would you want children to start learning real world skills? What ideas can you come up with that would speed up their learning so that they spend less time studying information they don't need? What courses would you introduce?

9. Passive Income

Create ten ideas you have for coming up with passive income ideas. What could you do for YouTube vids, writing an eBook, or creating an online course? Go to your main folder and dump in your ideas for passive income generation. I have already discussed building passive income so refer back to the previous chapter if necessary.

10. Personal Development and Character Building

What would you like to improve about yourself? Come up with at least thirty ideas for how you could deepen your character and personality? What would you have to do to make your personality a dynamic fit for any situation? What obstacles are challenging you these days? One of the areas that I am always trying to target is my confidence. When my confidence increases, I feel more motivated and excited to try just about anything.

11. Building Better Business

In this book we discussed ways to set up your ideas for building your own business. Now, what ideas do you have for creating a business? Write out all your ideas and then come up with action steps for your ideas using the strategies we discussed in this book. Do you want to create a business online? Do you want to expand on the current business you have?

12. Improving Relationships

Our relationships are precious gemstones. It's worth the time and effort to come up with at least fifty ideas on how you can build a relationship of better quality with your children, spouse, parents and relatives, and friends. What ideas can you map out right now that would add great value to these relationships?

13. Home Improvement

Can you come up with at least twenty ideas on how you could improve the look and feel of your home? What would you do to fix it up? What rooms would you repaint? Which areas need to be decluttered? Make a list of home improvement ideas. Then, set out to put just one idea into action. If you have to, map out any action steps necessary. Then, start to do the first task on your list.

14. Job Escape (Leaving Your Nine–Five)

Millions of people are unfulfilled in their work. They are looking for better ways to serve a higher purpose through doing work that matters. What if you could give that to them? Come up with ten ideas to create a plan for leaving a job you hate. Imagine that you are giving this as a presentation to people who have paid to hear you speak on this topic. What would you say?

Spend twenty minutes a day brainstorming creative ideas for anything that interests you. Your ideas are priceless; think of each idea as a brick in the success story of your life. You should add at least ten new "bricks" every day.

Remember this simple process when you are working on your ideas:

1. Mind map your ideas

2. Identify the actions you can take

3. Take immediate action

Putting Your Ideas to the Test

"New ideas pass through three periods: 1) It can't be done. 2) It probably can be done, but it's not worth doing. 3) I knew it was a good idea all along!"

— Arthur C. Clarke

Wouldn't it be great if we could get feedback on our ideas before we invested any time and money that could later turn out to be wasted? Would you like to know beforehand if your ideas are actually worth the effort?

Do others think your ideas are interesting? Test it. Tell them what you are planning and thinking about.

Here are three strategies I use to test my ideas first.

Ask Yourself: "Would I buy this service or product?"

You can test your idea by asking yourself if this is something you'd throw money down on. I test this idea with just about anything I create. If I write a book, before I do, I ask myself "Would I read this?" If it's a course or learning platform I am creating, I want to know "Would I sign up for this?" and if the answer is yes, come up with at least five solid reasons why.

This is a great way to really test it and, to be honest I think it's one of the best ways. When it comes to testing your idea and whether or not it would work, you are your most important customer. I wouldn't throw my money away on junk because I'm actually a very fussy shopper, and before I buy into a course, or even sign up for someone's website or blog, I ask "Is this what I want?"

If I look at my own "stuff" and there is strong hesitation, or I can't find a good reason to like it, chances are I'll have a tough sell expecting others to like it, not to mention spending money on it.

Let's take an example. You have an idea to create an online course. Test your idea by asking yourself:

"Would I buy this? If yes, why? If no, why not?

Would I recommend this this course to my friends?

If I had to describe this course, how would I explain it?

Do I get fired up when I talk about it?

Maybe not all of your ideas have to be this in depth but, if it's something that you are thinking of investing money in, you want to run it through a test drive first. It's like buying a new car: always take it for that initial test run.

Ask on Social Media

Nowadays it's easier than ever to put your ideas to the ultimate test. Ask the people you engage with on Facebook, Twitter, Instagram, LinkedIn, or your own emailing list if you have one. They will tell you the truth. I will use this as a second step if my idea passes my personal self-assessment.

Invite them to give you feedback or add their own thoughts to your ideas. Chances are, if your idea is a salable one, they will become just as excited as you are about it and add more depth to it by providing you with ideas of their own.

This is a great way to gain feedback and to investigate the 'worthiness' of what you are putting together. Be prepared for some critical feedback as well. Not everyone is going to as excited about the idea as you are. But that's okay, get used to receiving constructive criticism and you'll learn from it.

By telling others about your ideas and dreams, you could stimulate a conversation or a partnership leading to the development of a new revolutionary product or something that has never yet been tried. There is no telling what could happen once a group of people become interested in something you propose.

Before you know it, your idea has expanded into an image, the image becomes a plan, the plan becomes a detailed map, and that map becomes a plan of action.

Even if they think your idea is outrageous, that could be a compliment in disguise. Ideas are like dreams—they are not meant to exist in a one-dimensional world; they are multi-dimensional with unlimited possibilities.

Just Do It and Don't Worry About It

The last option is, I just *go for it.* Do what drives your passion and the hell with everything else. I'll be honest here: my own interests drive most of my ideas, and if it gets me fired up, I want to share that with everyone I know.

Just because you test an idea doesn't mean it's foolproof; some of the best creations are built on passion alone. In the end, it all comes down to what you feel strongly about doing; then you can do it the best you know how to and build anything you want from an idea driven by your energy.

Killing Your Doubt

Even if I like my ideas and I think it could be the next best thing to the Internet, doubt can cloud your judgment.

Do you know of anyone else who has had a similar idea? Can you build from their existing platform? Write down the first action step you are going to take right now to put this idea into motion.

Are there any reasons you think your idea is impossible? Make a list of these reasons. Now, challenge these reasons. Is it impossible because of lack of finances?

If so, how could you raise more money? Is it impossible because you lack the skills or know-how to put it into action? If so, who do you know that could help you? Is there any part of this that you could outsource to somebody else?

Make a list of resources. You could hire someone through Fiverr or Upwork. You might know of a friend who is willing to help you put it into action.

If your idea seems impossible, that is good. People have built their dreams and visions on impossible ideas that the rest of the world deemed crazy and were later accepted. So...

Put yourself out there.

Show the world what you've got.

If you feel good about what you are doing, do more of it.

Key Takeaways

- Test your ideas by asking yourself "would I buy this?
- Ask your friends and family close by what they really think of your plan.
- Reach out to people on social media sites that you regularly converse with and see what their feedback is. This can be a strong indicator that your idea is real.
- Take a survey using survey monkey or another online free resource.

Take Control of Your Life

"Your destiny is to fulfill those things upon which you focus most intently. So, choose to keep your focus on that which is truly magnificent, beautiful, uplifting and joyful. Your life is always moving toward something."

— Ralph Marston

I hope you enjoyed The Discipline of Masters and you are already implementing the action steps described within. As someone who lives by strategies, I like to share the best of what I can with my readers and coaching students to give them the greatest edge in a competitive world that is becoming increasingly demanding.

To get everything you have ever dreamed of, you have to do the things you never dreamed of. This has always been my motto. So, in this last part of the book, I'll leave you with a few final words.

Take Bold, Massive Action

You have undoubtedly heard that to move the dial on anything in your life requires a certain amount of action from you. This could be a commitment to something you do every day, such as the habit of exercising for twenty minutes every morning. Or, a commitment to work on your side business after you get home from work and put your kids to bed.

Gradually, after years of working, you make it. Massive action is total dedication to your mission. You decide when you will arrive at your destination instead of just letting the wind take you there. If you want to live a bold, fearless, freedom-rich lifestyle, you must be ready to take bold, massive action no matter what is going on in your life at the moment.

Turn Your Passion into a Creative Force

What do you feel such intense passion for that you would do anything to live like that every day? Imagine a life where you are your own master, you create what you want, and you share that creation with the people around you. How would your life change if you built this passion into your daily life, instead of trying to squeeze it into a busy lifestyle?

Passion is one of the greatest forces in the world because it can turn a good idea into a career. Passion is where dreams begin and boredom dies. Feeling bored with your life? You are not tapping into your passion. Frustrated, angry, or unsettled? That is good. These can be signs that you are seeking something greater.

Make Your Decision NOW

From today, there is one truth you need to know: the greatest change in your life is the power and the freedom to make a decision. If you want to start building your passion, start by making a decision that launches everything.

Find similar people who share your passion and work together to build something that changes the world or changes a group of people who go onto do great things.

Strive to Break Through Barriers

Remove your obstacles if you want this passion to grow. People are often held back by the problems, worry, and fears blocking growth. It is hard to live a passionate lifestyle when you are caught up in trivial issues. Refer back to section one for this.

Manage your actions and the rest will take care of itself. You don't need a bunch of goals for this. Just one goal to reach for that is a goal so big it has the power to change your life.

Be Thought Conscious

Your thoughts are powerful and govern your actions. So be aware of the critical thought processes you have. Are you in a situation where you are being negative? Does negative thinking pull you down? Do you meditate or practice any thought improvement exercises?

Now is the time to begin. Get moving on how to make things better. If things get better, how can you make them great? If everything is great, how you can make it fantastic? Then, go out and help someone else to do it.

As Zig Ziglar said, "If you help someone else get what they want, you will also get what you want."

So, go out and do this thing. Master your strategies and make a dent in the universe.

Don't wait for life to happen to you. Make it happen and bring the life you want toward you.

Until next time, be well.

Do what you love.

Help each other out.

Spend quiet time reflecting on your purpose and mission.

Don't settle for less.

Listen to what your heart wants.

The, go and do that thing.

All the best,

Scott Allan

“Sow an act and you reap a habit. Sow a habit and you reap a character. Sow a character and you reap a destiny.”

— James Allen